WRESTLING

RULES

FOR

LIFE

WRESTLING IS MORE THAN A SPORT
IT'S A LIFESTYLE

JOHNA PASSARO

To those who are in midst of a serious struggle,
Know, you are strong enough to endure.
To prosper.
To shine.
To give off light.

Table of Contents

FOR ALL PUBLISHED WORKS BY

JohnA Passaro

PLEASE GO TO:

www.johnapassarostore.com

It is easier to build strong children,
Then to repair broken men.

Frederick Douglas

CHAPTER 0

I never won a National Championship.

I have never been an All-American.

I never won a State Championship or even a Sectional Championship.

Heck, I don't even have cauliflower ear.

Not even on one ear.

But 36 years after wrestling my last match I still consider myself a wrestler.

That is because wrestling to me is more than a sport; it's a lifestyle.

For the longest time after my wrestling career ended I wanted nothing to do with the sport as I felt wrestling took everything I had and gave me back nothing in return.

I pledged I would never let my kids wrestle as I never wanted them to experience the pain that I experienced from this sport.

But, after 26 years, something brought me back.

And my kids did wrestle.

And when I had adversity in my life, I would come to realize that this sport has given back to me more than I could ever imagine.

It has taught me how to fight.

It has taught me to have an unbreakable will.

To be delusionally optimistic.

To bear unbearable adversity.

I've experienced this sport from every angle.

I was a wrestler myself for six years.

I've been a father of a wrestler for ten years.

I've been a father of a wrestling coach for three years.

I've been a coach all my life.

And I will forever be a fan of this sport.

Looking back over my time in this sport, it is clear to me that there are two types of former wrestlers.

Wrestlers who successfully bridged into life by applying the discipline and principles they learned on the mat, and those wrestlers who hadn't.

And the difference between the two is startling.

I noticed that it didn't matter what a wrestler's accolades were, each type of former wrestler existed at every level of success or non-success in the sport.

I was amazed at the disparity of the quality of life between the wrestlers who had applied the principals they lived on the mat and those who didn't.

The wrestlers who didn't apply the principals they learned on the mat seemed to be beaten by the exact principles wrestling had taught them.

How ironic.

It is like having the answers to the test before the test is given, then failing the test.

And then not even realizing why.

It baffles me.

I may not have racked up the accolades in this sport, but I do believe in the end I got the sport's greatest reward. I have been blessed with the understanding that wrestling is much more than a sport; it's a lifestyle.

That revelation has been invaluable to me in my life. It has made all the difference in the quality of my life.

So much so, that I feel compelled to share the principles that I've learned from this great sport. I hope that these principles will sound familiar and ring true to wrestlers who need them the most.

Champions on the mat in the sport who now need help off the mat in life.

JohnA Passaro

Rule #1
Don't Beat Yourself

To see a man beaten
Not by a better opponent
But by himself
Is a tragedy.
Cus D'Amato

You will reach a point in time in your life when you will stop wrestling.

It is at that time life will become your new opponent.

Life will be the most formidable opponent you will ever face.

No amount of training will ever prepare you for the onslaught that life has in store for you.

To win in life, as in wrestling, you must first learn not to beat yourself.

A new wrestler learns not to beat himself by eliminating putting himself in bad positions and by deciding never to do anything that exposes his back.

In life, you must first learn to do the same.

Having a great stance in wrestling is of paramount importance in the process of learning how not to beat yourself.

A great wrestling stance has three lines of defense:

The head, the hands, and the hips.

Each line of defense is designed to protect the most valuable parts of a wrestler's body from attack from his opponent.

Never breaking stance is key to a wrestler's success on the wrestling mat.

In your battle against life, your new stance is your lifestyle.

A great lifestyle will keep you out of bad positions.

A great lifestyle will keep your back from being exposed.

A great lifestyle will stop life from scoring easy points on you.

A great lifestyle has three lines of defense
your mind, your body, and your spirit.

They will always be under attack by life.

Decide early on not to partake in any activity,
especially the use of drugs, alcohol or the reliance on
any chemical that will change the state of your brain,
as it will inevitably and undoubtedly diminish your
mind, deteriorate your body, and evaporate your
spirit.

Thus putting you in a bad position and exposing
your back to life.

Living a clean lifestyle is the fundamental building
block to sustained happiness and success in life.

You must never break your lifestyle.

As soon as you do, life will take you down.

And if you happen to break your lifestyle and life
doesn't take you down, well, that outcome is even
worse.

Mistakenly, you will feel that your lifestyle is not as important in stopping the attack from life.

You wouldn't be more wrong.

Your lifestyle must protect the three most valuable areas in your life; your mind, your body, and your spirit.

You need your mind to make good decisions, your body to be in ultimate health, and the fortitude of your spirit to win verse life.

Imagine for a moment that you are in a wrestling match verse a highly trained, extremely motivated opponent.

An opponenet that is not only looking to beat you but looking to annihilate and humiliate you in the process.

For a few years of your life, that opponent will be the competition lining up across the circle from you.

For decades after wrestling, life will be that opponent.

Have you ever been thrown to your back early in a period in a wrestling match and had to fight off your back for the entire two minutes to not get pinned?

It's not a fun thing to have to do.

It takes a lot of energy to survive and stay in the match.

Now, imagine getting thrown to your back early in life and having to spend the next ten, twenty, or even sixty years fighting, trying not to get pinned.

With the full faculty of your mind, the health of your body and a razor-sharp spirit, you will have the tools needed to beat life.

With any portion of your mind, your body or your spirit at less than full capacity you will undoubtedly give up easy points to life, put yourself in bad positions and ultimately life will throw you to your back.

Life is too skilled of an opponent to attempt to beat with anything less than your best.

If there is anything in your lifestyle that makes you vulnerable to giving up easy points to life, it is imperative that you immediately drop everything and direct your full attention to making the necessary corrections.

Do not go on to any other rules until those necessary corrections have been made, as no matter what you do if you do not master Rule #1, "Don't Beat Yourself," mastering all the other rules will prove fruitless.

There is nothing more important to the quality of your life than living a clean lifestyle.

As Cus D'Amato, the former trainer to Mike Tyson so prophetically said,

"To see a man beaten, not by a better opponent but by himself, is a tragedy."

RULE #2
DREAM BIG DREAMS

There is nothing like a dream
To create the future.
Victor Hugo
Les Misérables

Magic is made when you dream big dreams.

To reach a goal bigger than you thought you could ever accomplish, you will need to become someone greater than you ever thought you could be.

And that is the magic.

The magic of your unique personal transformation into the best version of yourself.

The power of the magic begins with the audacity to believe you can and will accomplish your biggest dream.

When you believe, you will become a first-hand witness to the Universe, through trials, tribulations, adversity, and setbacks, forge you into a diamond.

Know, the bigger the dream, the greater the journey.

The greater the journey, the deeper the transformation.

So, dream.

Then have the audacity to dream even bigger.

As a big dream will necessitate taking inventory of assets and tapping into resources you never knew existed.

A big dream will force you to use everything at your disposal.

It will require hard work and commitment.

It will require tenacity and persistence.

It will require getting back up more times than you have been knocked down.

It will not be easy.

The journey will test your preconceived limits.

There will be times that you will curse the journey.

Understand, that is also the precise point when the alchemy of your transformation is taking place.

So, overcome the obstacles you never thought you were able to be overcome.

Put dedication and perseverance to work.

The journey is the process that makes the man.

The bigger the dream.

The greater the journey.

The better the finished man.

So, dream big dreams.

Greatness is waiting for you.

It is inside you beckoning for you to call upon it.

Make the call.

Dig down deep into your reservoir of belief you never knew existed and allow the magic of dreaming big dreams transform you into the best version of yourself.

Live life as Walt Whitman once profoundly wrote,

"From this hour, I ordain myself loosed of limits and imaginary boundaries."

And watch your life blossom.

RULE #3
BELIEVE BEFORE

We know what we are,
But not what we may be.
Shakespeare

Have you ever wrestled an opponent you knew was better than you?

I bet you didn't wrestle like yourself at the beginning of the match.

I bet you were hesitant; you didn't react the same, you let opportunities pass you by, you allowed your opponent to recover from errors without consequence.

And I bet somewhere mid-2nd period you said to yourself,

"What am I doing? I could go with this guy."

By that time, though, it was too late as half the match was over.

I bet after the match you said to yourself,

"If I only wrestled like myself right from the beginning, I know I could have won that match."

The key to beating someone better than yourself is to believe that you can way before you get confirmation that you are correct in your thinking.

To believe before confirmation, you need to trust yourself.

You need to trust in your talent, your work ethic, your dedication, and your perseverance.

Trust is the cousin to belief.

When trust and belief team up, they don't require outside confirmation they thrive on inside collaboration.

When trust and belief team up, their ears are deaf to the words "can't."

Their eyes don't need to see it done before.

Their heart knows.

Trust in the belief in your heart.

Believe in your trust.

****

Shakespeare wrote,

"We know what we are, but not what we may be."

The most important people in your life are the people who believe in you before confirmation of their intuition.

These people will have the biggest impact on your life.

They see something in you, way before you even see it in yourself.

Always keep these people in your life at any cost.

Give them a perpetual place in your inner circle.

Hold them in a special place in your heart.

Better yet, learn from them and become one of them.

And start to see in others what they haven't yet seen in themselves.

And in the process, you will teach them to do the same.

RULE #4
BE YOURSELF

This above all else,
To thine own self be true
Shakespeare

One of the reasons why wrestling is such a great sport is because there is no prototypical body type needed for success.

There are many different body types in wrestling, and all can be successful.

There is the long and lean, the short and stocky, the athletic body, the unassuming.

There are too many to list them all.

Each body type has its unique strengths and weaknesses.

The wrestler who uses their body type to the best of their ability develops a style unique to their own.

One of the keys to success in wrestling is to utilize the resources given to you for their maximum benefit.

If you are long and lean, then legs and cradles will be moves you should learn to master.

If you are short and stocky, then double legs will be beneficial to master.

The biggest mistake a wrestler can make is to emulate a successful wrestler who has a different body type as they do.

If you want to emulate a successful wrestler, emulate the fact that they used their body type to their maximum advantage and developed a style that was unique to their own.

Do the same.

Take your body type and use it to your advantage and develop a style unique to you, and success will follow.

****

In life, there is no prototypical way to achieve success.

There are many paths which lead to success.

Every person in life has different circumstances.

Every person has different resources.

Emulate a person who came from similar circumstances as your own, with similar resources and learn from their success.

When you study success, the individuals who maximize their unique strengths and utilize all resources available to them often become successful.

Learn to use your uniqueness and success will follow.

****

Ralph Waldo Emerson succinctly said,

"Insist on yourself; never imitate.
Your own gift you can present every moment with
the cumulative force of a whole life's cultivation;
but of the adopted talent of another, you have only
an extemporaneous half possession.
That which each can do best, none but his Maker can
teach him."

Rule #5
Nobody Can Want It More for You Than You Want It for Yourself

None of us will ever accomplish
Anything excellent or commanding
Except when he listens to this whisper
Which is heard by him alone.
Emerson

Is "your dream" more important to someone else than it is to you?

If it is, I hate to tell you it is not your dream.

It is theirs.

If you answered that your dream is more important to someone else; your dad, your coach, your brother, anyone else, you may have initial success, but there will reach a point when the other person wants you to do things you are unwilling to do.

To reach down deeper than you care too.

To sacrifice more than you want.
At that point, you will meet resistance.

And unless you want it more than anyone else wants it for you, resistance will win.

And the law of deterioration will be set in motion.

Resentment will set in when the difference of what others want from you and what you want for yourself collide.

At first, the battles will be small, but they will quickly escalate in time.

And one day they will come to a head.

You can't "wrestle/live your life" for your parents. You can't "wrestle/live your life" for your coach. You can't "wrestle/live your life" for your brother, teammates or friend.

You can only "wrestle/live your life" for yourself.

When you do and reach an obstacle that requires you to reach deep down, you will.

There will be no resistance.

Rule #6
The Odds Should Be Respected But Not Believed

Impossible odds
Set the stage
For amazing miracles.
Jentezen Franklin

Never let the odds be a deterrent to the achievement of your dream.

As the odds are just other people's success rate at what you are looking to accomplish yourself.

They are not your odds.

Understand many others have attempted and failed at what you are trying to accomplish, so you need to respect the difficulty that lies ahead.

Realize, in other people's failure, they lacked something in their effort, their makeup, their endurance.

That is why they failed.

You need to study and learn from other people's failures; take and use what worked for them and improve upon what did not.

Find what they were missing.

Perhaps it is something you possess?

Add your uniqueness to the mix, as your uniqueness may be the exact missing ingredient the others did not have and just may have been the reason they did not accomplish the task.

Abraham Lincoln wisely said,

"Always bear in mind that your own resolution to succeed is more important than any other."

Always remember that the odds to accomplish anything in life are like seeds for a tournament or rankings during the season, they are just somebody else's opinion of what they think should happen.

Other people's opinions don't matter unless you let them.

If you let other people's opinion throw shade on your vision, your confidence, or your action taking; then their opinion will become a self-fulfilling prophecy.

For them.

Don't let other people's opinion carry any weight in your vision.

Your own opinion is the only one that matters.

I have never met a wrestler who was ranked 2nd who didn't believe he could win a championship.
I have never met an unranked wrestler who didn't believe he belonged on the rankings board.
This is what drives them to succeed.

The only opinion that truly matters is your own.

****

I have done some research.

I live in Suffolk County, Long Island.

Section XI to be exact.

A hotbed for wrestling.

Section XI has won the New York State Division 1 Wrestling Tournament ten of the past eleven years.

It is wrestling heaven.

Wrestling is taken seriously, here.

It is followed ferociously.

Section XI knows wrestling.

Even with all the passion, all the coverage, all the history, research has shown that the preseason rankings accurately forecast that years Sectional XI Champions approximately 40% of the time.

That means they are inaccurate 60% of the time.

Always remember the only rankings that truly matter are the results at the end of the season.

Everything else is noise designed to distract you.

RULE #7
BE DELUSIONALLY OPTIMISTIC

There is a fine line
Between
Genius and insanity.
Oscar Levant

Your mind is magical.

It can accomplish anything you set it to accomplish.

When your mind is coupled with hard work, grit, and perseverance, it can produce results far beyond anyone's wildest expectations.

Even your own.

Your mind is also logical.

Nothing magical ever happens while being logical.

Scott Green, the head wrestling coach of Wyoming Seminary once profoundly wrote,

"Life is 90% reason, rationality, discipline, and organization.
You need to live your life that way.
That last 10% is a leap of faith, an emotional connection, an irrational belief.
That last 10% makes no sense at all.
But the truth is, nothing worth having and nothing worth accomplishing, happens without that last part.
You have to live in that world to do something great."

There is a time and a place for logic.

It's just not in your suitcase on your journey to greatness.

It will slow you down.

Pack magic in your suitcase instead.

It will be the wind at your back.

****

The magic begins when you make a declaration to yourself that you are going to do extraordinary things despite the obvious overwhelming obstacles in your way.

When you make this declaration to yourself, your mind will immediately set two points.

Point A is where you are.

Point B is where you want to be, what you want to accomplish.

Immediately after setting the two points your subconscious mind will perform its magic and map out its journey.

And soon after, the whole Universe will aid you in unforeseen ways to connect the two points in your journey.

The starting point of magic requires you to be irrational.

Oscar Levant said,

"There is a fine line between genius and insanity."

To believe despite the obstacles, the problems, the challenges, the headwinds requires getting extremely close to the line of insanity.

The closest one can come to that insanity line without touching it, is called delusional optimism.

Delusional optimism is the 10% leap of faith, the emotional connection, the irrational belief needed to accomplish anything worthwhile.

Delusional optimism is powerful.

It reduces obstacles into solvable problems.

It provides the grit when logic says to quit.

Delusional optimism draws on all resources necessary to believe during discouraging plateaus and persevere during adversity.

I believe being sane is sometimes the biggest mistake people make in their lives.
As Dale Wasserman wrote in Man of La Mancha,

"Too much sanity may be madness, and maddest of all: to see life as it is, and not as it should be."

****

I remember where I was when I heard Austin DeSanto had beaten Spencer Lee on a last-second takedown in the 2017 Pennsylvania High School State Championships.

Hearing the results was surreal, something unbelievable to comprehend at the time as Spencer Lee, the reigning 3x State Champion, not only teched DeSanto in the state finals the prior year but was also undefeated throughout his entire high school career with a record of 144-0 going into the match.

A few minutes after I had heard that Austin DeSanto had beaten Spencer Lee, it dawned on me that DeSanto had made a declaration earlier in the year that he was going to beat Spencer Lee and win a Pennsylvania State Championship.

At the time, I thought he was delusional.

I was wrong; he was delusionally optimistic.

There is a difference.

No matter what you may think of Austin DeSanto's antics since that time, his 2017 State Championship, defeating Spencer Lee in the process, is one of the greatest examples of the magical power of delusional optimism I have ever witnessed in the sport of wrestling.

Delusional optimism backed by hard work, grit, and perseverance is the formula for magic.

The Persian Poet Rumi best defined delusional optimism when he said,

"To live life as though everything is rigged in your favor."

What a way to live life.

Rule #8
Have The And 1 Attitude

If I were to wish for anything,
I should not wish for wealth or power,
But for an eye that sees the possible.
Soren Kierkegaard

One can learn a tremendous amount from failure.

And even more from success.

When a wrestler with a 50-1 record is introduced, what does your mind focus on?

Is your mind intimidated by the 50 opponents he beat or does the 1 opponent who beat him give you hope and a plan?

Be attracted to what aids you to be victorious.

Train your mind to think,

"Who was the And 1 and what did he do differently than the other 50 wrestlers who failed in attempting to beat him?"

There was something that the "And 1" did that the others could not.

There was a certain way the "And 1" handled situations that the others did not.

There was some reason the "And 1" ended up on top when the others did not.

Train your eye to find the small details that made the "And 1" different than everyone else.

****

In everything you do in life, there will be 50 reasons why you shouldn't do it, and one reason why you should.

Always focus on the one reason why you should.

RULE #9
EVERYTHING MATTERS

Your beliefs become your thoughts,
Your thoughts become your words,
Your words become your actions,
Your actions become your habits,
Your habits become your values,
Your values become your destiny.
Gandhi

Water boils at 212 degrees.

At 211 degrees, water is just hot.

Every degree is needed to bring water to combustion.

If even one degree doesn't do its job, water will not boil, it will just remain hot.

I attest that we all have 212 degrees to make our lives boil.

Every degree Is needed to bring our lives to combustion.

I attest that at 211 degrees our lives are just hot.

I attest there are no small things in life.
Each one degree can be the missing catalyst to your
life boiling or being just hot.

Every degree matters.

****

Imagine that your goal is this mountain in the
distance ahead of you, and you desire to get to this
mountain within the next four years.

In everything that you do during your journey
towards the mountain ask yourself,

"Is what I am about to do going to take me closer to
the mountain, or is it going to take me further away
from it?"

If the answer is that it is going to take you closer to
the mountain, you do it.

If it takes you even one inch further from the
mountain, you don't.

It is that simple.

By eliminating the things in your life that takes you further from your goal, you immediately become closer to your goal.

****

In wrestling, everything matters.

Every pound matters.
Every second matters.
Every point matters.
Every day matters.

Everything matters.

In life, everything matters.

Every second matters.
Every day matters.
Every word matters.
Every dollar matters.

Everything matters.

On each attempt and subsequent failure, you are writing your algorithm for success.

RULE #10
LIVE IN THE ZONE

Good and great
Are seldom in the same man.
Winston S. Churchill

Cracker Barrel has a hand-held game where the object of the game is to roll a small ball into a tiny hole by minutely tilting the board it is on in different directions.

It looks easy.

Until you attempt it.

And when you do, no matter how precise your tilt of the board may be, the ball will get close to the hole and carom away.

It takes many, many attempts to get the tilt just right so the ball falls into the hole.

After many attempts and lots of frustration, your tilt will be just right, your poise and balance will be exactly appropriate, and the ball will magnetically roll into the hole.

That is the best description of The Zone.

The Zone is the time and place in life where everything comes together perfectly.

It is where good transitions into great.

****

The Zone is a self-made state of massive production.

It is where focus, work, and time combine for phenomenal results.

It is the place where everything goes your way; every break, every call, every roll of the ball, it all goes your way.

The Zone is an extremely rare state, one which is most difficult to get into.

You get "In the Zone" by having extreme focus, discipline, and perseverance.

You get "In the Zone" when you keep pushing good to become great.

Once you arrive "In the Zone" you must preserve your time there like a rodeo rider attempting to stay on a bucking horse for as long as he can.

Every second counts.

Every experience counts.

Time and experience are prerequisites for entry into The Zone.

On each attempt and subsequent failure, you are writing your algorithm for success.

Each attempt becomes better than your last as failure supplies new information for you to incorporate in your next attempt.

With each attempt and subsequent failure, good is getting one step closer to becoming great.

How many attempts will be needed to have good become great?

That is unknown.

But there is an amount.

The challenge is to walk with the unknown until the known is revealed.

Learn to be comfortable in the unknown.

As its mastery is vital to your success.

Thrive in it.

As it will lead you to The Zone.

Where good gets turned into great.

Rule #11
Surround Yourself With Great People With Like-Minded Goals

You are the average of the five people
You spend the most time with.
Jim Rohn

Imagine you are part of an experiment where you must relinquish your thoughts and your decision-making process to someone in your life for a full month.

And the goal is that after a month you must be closer to your goal than before the month started.

Now go through every person you associate with in your life and ask yourself,

"Would I trust that responsibility to anyone?"

If your answer is no, then you got some cleaning house to do.

If the answer is yes, that's your inner circle.

That's your alliance.

Those are the people you keep in your life.

You might say this experiment may seem far-fetched, that you will never allow anyone in your life to 100% think for you or to make all decisions for you.

I beg to differ.

There will be a time in your life when you will not be at your best, and you will have to rely on those closest to you for guidance.

They will influence you.

For good or for bad.

Choose wisely who you associate with as one day they may be the one asked to take life's wheel for you.

RULE #12
FEED THE GOOD

Your life is your garden,
Your thoughts are your seeds.
If your life isn't awesome,
You have been watering the weeds.
Terry Prince

Every person alive has chatter inside their heads.

Some of it is good, some of it bad.

We don't get to choose the chatter.

But we do get to choose which chatter becomes louder.

The chatter that becomes louder will be the chatter that you feed.

Henry David Thoreau put it this way,

"As a single footstep will not make a path on the earth, so, a single thought will not make a pathway in the mind.

To make a deep physical path, we need to walk again and again.

To make a deep mental path, we must think over and over the kind of thoughts we wish to dominate our lives."

Your brain is miraculous.

Inside your brain are good thoughts that will steer your life.

Your job is to find them and feed them.

RULE #13
PICK THE RIGHT PARTNER

For he today,
That sheds his blood with me,
Shall always be my brother.
Shakespeare
Henry V

There is nothing more important in wrestling and life than to pick the right partner.

The right partner is someone who has the same beliefs, the same value system, and the same lifestyle as you.

It is someone who brings out the best in you.

It is someone willing to bleed alongside you.

****

The greatest partnerships in wrestling and marriage are two people who make each other better in their journey to make themselves better.

Not two people who are solely trying to make themselves better.

Not one person becoming better at the detriment of the other.

But rather, two people who both become better because of their alliance to the same goal.

Partnerships break down, and marriages fail when one partner feels the other is not reciprocating in making the other better, they have shifted their focus, concentrating only on making themselves better.

They become a taker and not a giver.

A taker takes, and that only lasts for a certain period. A giver receives, and that goes on forever.

One of the greatest lessons in wrestling and marriage is learning that the partnership is about making both partners better. They make you better, and you make them better.

It is not a partnership if only one-party benefits.

The partnership needs to benefit both partners.

****

The only time in life when you get to choose your family is in marriage.

Everyone knows the wedding vows,

For better, for worse
For richer, for poorer
In sickness and in health.

How do you know you have the right partner in life?

When you have been dealt,
For worse, for poorer and in sickness and you still consider yourself lucky because you realize it is not what you go through in life; it is who you go through life with.

Shakespeare wrote in Henry V,

"For he today, that sheds his blood with me, shall always be my brother."

Competition with losses against elite opponents is more valuable than competition without losses against inferior opponents.

RULE #14
IRON SHARPENS IRON

As iron sharpens iron,
So, one person sharpens another.
Proverbs 27:17

Rivals bring out the best in you.

They make you train harder; they make you obsess over the details, the small things, the important things.

They require you to be at your best or pay the price.

The process of seeking out, training, and preparing for the best competition will push you, drive you, inspire you.

It will sharpen you.

****

When asked if he would rather fight against the best fighters or be undefeated, the legendary Sugar Ray Leonard responded with these wise words,

"They think being 25-0 means something.
It doesn't mean anything.
It's okay to have two or three losses.
It's what kind of fighter you are that the people respect.
I have a few losses on my record, but that doesn't justify who I am.
Hearn's had losses.
Duran had losses.
Hagler had losses.
That made us better fighters."

Competition with losses against elite opponents is more valuable than competition without losses against inferior opponents.

RULE #15
MAKE YOUR TEAMMATES BETTER

We're a team.
One person struggles; we all struggle.
One person triumphs; we all triumph.
Coach Carter

It is so easy to get caught up thinking that wrestling is an individual sport.

It is, but it also happens to be one of the greatest team sports in existence.

In wrestling, your teammates are your coaches, your workout partners, your family, your fans, and your mentors.

They are all there to make you better.

Your success, in a small way, is their success.

Your pain is their pain.

Your growth is their growth.

****

One day wrestling will be over.

And your new opponent will be life.

And your new teammates will be your family.

In life, the greatest team you will ever be on will be your family.

And the most important family member will be the one who makes everyone around them better.

The one during times of crisis holds everyone together.

The one who at the lowest level of hope has the highest degree of belief.

Every family member is an individual within the team.

That's what wrestling is.

That's what being part of a family is.

That's what being part of a community is.

That's what being part of a country is.

As Timo Cruz said in Coach Carter,

"We're a team. One person struggles; we all struggle. One person triumphs, we all triumph."

The ability to treat every person you meet with kindness, whether they are the janitor or the CEO of a major company, will allow you to learn from everyone in life.

RULE #16
BE COACHABLE

You must always be
The apprentice.
Even when you become
The master.
Christopher Cumby

Whether you think you can learn from everyone,
or whether you think you are too good to learn from
anyone; you will be right.

Wouldn't you rather be right increasing your
knowledge rather than restricting it?

Don't cut off your ability to learn or limit from
where your education will come.

I believe, how coachable you are as an athlete will
dictate how you will see people in life.

If you feel you can learn something from everyone,
your outlook on people in life will be vastly different
than if you feel there is nobody you could learn
from.

The ability to treat every person you meet with kindness, whether they are the janitor or the CEO of a major company, will allow you to learn from everyone in life.

Every person alive has a story worth telling.
A story worth hearing.
A story worth sharing.

Listen to people's stories, and your life will be better for it.
Hear their trials and tribulations, their moments of glory, how they overcome adversity.
Meet the people they love and learn the reasons why they do.

Be curious.

Learn from other people's lives, and your life will be fuller for doing so.

Be open to the fact that every person on this earth can teach you something.

And you will find, they will.

RULE #17
EARNED NOT GIVEN

Luck is not chance,
It's toil.
Fortune's expensive smile is
Earned.
Emily Dickinson

The current millennial generation is known for its sense of entitlement.

Wrestlers are known for their work ethic and their ability to earn their way.

Wrestling should be a mandatory course in life.

It would solve a lot of problems our society is currently facing.

If I were creating the curriculum for the mandatory wrestling course for life, it would look like this:

Wrestling & Life 101 – Set a goal, have a vision.

Wrestling & Life 102 – Create a plan.

Wrestling & Life 103 – Attempt to execute the plan.

Wrestling & Life 104 – Fail in your attempt to execute the plan.

Wrestling & Life 105 – Persevere through discouragement and disappointment with action and passion.

Wrestling & Life 106 – Rest and restart with a newly revised plan.

Wrestling & Life 107 – Keep making adjustments to the plan until the plan is nearly flawless.

Wrestling & Life 108 – Execute in the big spot.

Wrestling & Life 109 – Be humble, have gratitude, give back.

Wrestling & Life 110 – Set your sight on a new goal, with a new vision.

RULE #18
HARD WORK WINS

Short cuts
Make long delays.
J.R.R. Tolkien
The Fellowship of the Ring

It is a very simple formula.

Do the work.

Put in the time.

Learn.

Apply.

And eventually, you will achieve your goals.

If you haven't yet achieved your goals, work harder, put in more time, be smarter, and apply better.

Become wiser and more efficient with each passing day.

In "The Divine Comedy," Dante wrote,

"The path to paradise begins in hell."

Whenever you find yourself in a position of reflection of why you haven't yet met your goals, the corrective action to take will be simple.

Get back to work.

Work harder.

Work smarter.

Put in more time.

Learn from your mistakes and failures.

Apply what you learned.

And then it won't be if, but only a matter of time before you succeed.

RULE #19
Nobody Outworks You

There may be people that have more talent than you,
But there is no excuse
For anyone to work harder than you do.
Derek Jeter

Wrestlers are known for their work ethic.

It is what separates them from others in real life.

It is a great feeling knowing you the hardest worker in the room.

It is a characteristic most sought after by many employers.

It is the reason why wrestlers make great employees.

I've worked for companies who only hired athletes, especially wrestlers because they knew their work ethic would be supreme.

Many things are out of your control.

Your ability to be the hardest worker in the room is not one of them.

Take pride in the fact that nobody will ever outwork you.

Rule #20
Your Confidence
Will be in Direct Proportion
To Your Preparedness

Every position is my best position.
Kyle Dake

Confidence is best defined as a belief in oneself.

Having a belief in oneself is attributed to knowing.

Knowing comes from being prepared.

Preparation comes from putting in the work, making the sacrifices and experiencing the pain.

Confidence is vital to achievement.

Confidence is binary.

There is no middle ground.

Either you have it, or you don't.

There is no such thing as being "a little bit confident."

Confidence cannot be faked.

It can only be earned.

Confidence is earned through hard work,
extreme sacrifice, and by enduring physical pain.

Then, and only then will you be prepared,
and then and only then will you have confidence.

Every test you face where you do the work,
make the sacrifice, and absorb the pain of struggle,
is recorded by your mind.

The results are stored deep in your subconscious.

When your confidence is called upon, immediately
your subconscious mind will become the judge and
jury and will determine if you deserve its delivery
based on those prior test results.

There is an old saying that you can't fool yourself.

When earned, confidence will be at your beckoning
call.

When you convince your subconscious mind that you have properly prepared, sacrificed, and have handled the pain, confidence will automatically appear.

And you will be rewarded by its presence.

The outcome isn't the goal.

Your output is.

RULE #21
99% EFFORT IS NOT ENOUGH

The important thing is
That those 20 boys know in 20 years,
They didn't leave anything on the table.
They played their hearts out.
That's the important thing.
Herb Brooks
Coach of 1980 US Hockey Team

Imagine that you are shopping for life insurance to protect your family, who are the most important thing in the world to you.

There is a one-million-dollar policy that costs $1,000 a year and covers your family every day of the year.

There is another one-million-dollar policy which only costs $500 a year but doesn't cover your family on Fridays; if you were to die on a Friday, the policy wouldn't payout to your family.

Which one would you choose?

Sounds silly right?

Why would someone care enough to take out life insurance but leave themselves vulnerable on Fridays?

It may not be as important as life insurance for your family, but only giving 99% effort towards your goal is the same thing.

Why would you care enough to do 99% only to leave yourself vulnerable by the 1% left undone?

Once it was all said and done, and my wrestling career was over, and I had time to reflect, I realized a major lesson in my wrestling journey was learning to give my all.

100% of it.

Not holding back.

Learning to be all in.

All the time.

No matter what.

Having no vulnerabilities in effort.

I was best able to give 100% by concentrating on what was important and learning to control what I could control.

To not be distracted by the constant noise of life.

Always being on an ongoing journey towards my vision.

When I did that, I was able to live with any outcome, because I knew I did everything I could, there wasn't one more thing I possibly could have done.

And, then and only then, could I live with any, and all, results.

With no regret.

One of the greatest lessons I have learned from the sport of wrestling is that the outcome isn't the goal.

Your output is.

You can't control the outcome.

You can control your output.

The goal is to give 100% of what you have.

And then you can live with any outcome.

100% effort kills regret.

If you give 99%, your peace of mind will be vulnerable for life.

For every 1% that you hold back, is an additional 1% chink in your armor.

For every 1% that you hold back is 1% that goes in your opponent's opportunity column.

So, don't hold back.

Don't pace yourself.

Don't save some for later.

Why in the world would you be willing to do 99% and then not be willing to do 1% more?

Most people leave the remaining 1% undone because the last 1% is tolling.

The truth is it requires much more effort than it numerically suggests.

There are very few people willing to do significantly more work than 1% to only get 1% in return.

It seems like an unfair trade.

I'm telling you to gladly pay significantly more for the final 1%.

Because what people fail to realize is that last 1% returns to you so much more.

It takes you to a new level.

If you have been fastidious enough to give to 99% effort, one, give yourself credit and then two, go back to work to give the other 1%.

All you can give is all that you have.

Give it all.

And you will always be at peace with yourself.

Only you know if you deserve the special force stored in your soul.

RULE #22
You Can't Fool Yourself

Your brain will not sow lies,
And then reap the truth.

There is a saying in life,

"You can't run from yourself."

You are the only person with yourself 100% of the time.

Only you know if your toe touched the line when running suicides.

Only you know if you had more to give after the final whistle blew.

Only you know if you deserve the special force stored in your soul when you are reaching down for more.

Most people don't have confidence because they feel that they don't deserve it.

Why?

They know everything about themselves,
and they know what they did, what they didn't do,
and their subconscious mind made an evaluation
that they didn't deserve success.

Other people know they have done all that was
asked of them, and when they reached down to get
more, it is delivered because their subconscious
made an evaluation and determined that they
earned it.

Be in harmony with success by doing the work.

Convince the judge and jury, your subconscious
mind, that you deserve success.

And success will appear.

Rule #23
Give Everything
Or Get Nothing

You find that you have peace of mind
And can enjoy yourself,
Get more sleep, and rest,
When you know
That it was a one hundred percent effort
That you gave,
Win or lose.
Geordie Howe

Most people have what it takes, but they are not willing to give everything they got.

When you give everything you got, there will be a time where you will have nothing left, and you are left vulnerable.

I attest it is in this state of vulnerability that desperation arises.

The feeling of desperation is vital to ignite one into the relentless action needed to overcome all obstacles.

The feeling of having nothing left creates a desire to get everything back.

And more.

So, don't hold back.

Not even a little.

Give everything.

Without giving everything,

You get to keep the little you didn't give.

And in the scheme of things, that is nothing.

You need to have a gear that others, don't have.

The desperation gear.

If at this moment that gear eludes you,
then there is nothing more important than obtaining
it.

Right now.

Above all else.

For it is in that unpopulated gear where the jewels are stored.

The desperation gear originates in desire.

Only you, and you alone can desire an outcome you are willing to fight for.

To sacrifice for.

To bleed for.

To give all you have for.

To reach your zone of vulnerability and un-comfortability for.

Without the guarantee of success.

It takes a feeling of desperation to know all you want is just outside of your reach and that an extra effort is needed, one even above the already insane output of energy you have already exalted.

It's the same feeling of funneled focused desperation as when you are rope training, giving 100% output, but somehow "you will" the rope faster.

It isn't your physical fitness which makes the rope go faster; it's your desperate desire to create a new maximum output that does.

With vulnerability comes desperation.

With desperation comes relentlessness.

And with relentlessness comes achievement.

RULE #24
GET 1% BETTER EVERY DAY

Little by little, one travels far.
J.R.R. Tolkien

There are approximately 100 days in the high school wrestling season.

If a high school wrestler commits to getting
1% better every day, by the end of the season,
they will double their stamina, their technique, and
their effectiveness.

Most people feel there isn't enough time in the day.

Not having enough time isn't the issue.

The issue is utilizing the time you do have more efficiently.

No one gets to increase the amount of time they have.

We can only more efficiently utilize the time that we have.

Practice with a purpose.

Slow and steady wins the race.

Consistency wins.

Take the approach life is not a sprint;
it is a marathon.

Small gains over long periods.

Life is the same way.

Life has many 100-day periods, more than three per
year.

Get 1% better each day in every area of your life.

Be productive.

Make small gains every day over long periods.

The Roman Stoic philosopher Seneca said it best,

"It is not that we have so little time.

The life we receive is not short, but we make it so;
We are not ill provided but use what we have
wastefully."

Be jealous of your time.

Use it effectively.

Seek to get 1% better every day.

Touch someone's soul, every day

RULE #25
DO YOUR EVERYDAY'S EVERY DAY

Your life is a sculpture.
Chip away,
Every day.
J.R. Rim

Greatness begins when practice ends.

It is not what you do during a scheduled practice which makes you great.

It is what you do after one that does.

Early in his career, an elite wrestler will realize that the scheduled practice will only take him so far.

That if he wants to get better, he must work on fundamentals and techniques that are specific to his success on his own after practice.

Every wrestler has moves and defenses that he will use in a match.

These moves and defenses must be mastered.

Singles, mat returns, single defense, leg defense…

After their mastery, these techniques and skills must be kept sharp by drilling them every day.

There is not enough time in practice for everyone to drill their specific moves, defenses, and technique.

They must be done individually, on your own time.

After practice, you will see the great ones take an extra twenty minutes to drill the techniques that are vital to their success.

To keep them sharp.

I call this extra practice – "Everyday's."

To keep their mastery, they must be drilled every day.

*****

In his infamous ESPY speech, a dying Jimmy Valvano said,

"To me, there are three things everyone should do every day.

Number one is laugh.

Number two is think. Spend some time in thought.

Number three, you should have your emotions move you to tears. It could be happiness or joy.

But think about it, if you laugh, think and cry, that's a heck of a day.

If you do that seven days a week, you are going to be special."

Here are Everydays for life.

Do something for someone who has no way of repaying you, every day.

Say "I Love You," to the people that you care about, every day.

Say,

"I'm sorry,"
"Thank you,"
"I believe in you,"
"I'm here for you,"
"I'll be right over,"

Every day.

Amaze someone who thinks they know you best, every day.

Touch someone's soul, every day.

Listen intently to your soul, every day.

Appreciate from your core the life that you have been given, every day.

Find gratitude, even when, especially when the circumstances are such that gratitude doesn't seem to be warranted.

Getting in your life's, "Everyday's," every day, is what makes life great.

Rule #26
Push Beyond Your Limits Daily

Push me past my limit all you want.
It's territory I know all too well.
Ben Greenhalgh

The average human uses only 10% of their brain.

That means we have 10x more mind function to tap into.

Imagine if your brain was 10x smarter,
10x more effective, 10x more efficient than it was at your greatest moment?

The possibilities of achievement are limitless.

The common person, though, stays within the 10% that he has always used never going beyond the misconstrued boundaries of their mind;
in essence, creating a self-imposed fence around future achievement.

Go beyond the boundaries.

Unleash the 10x force.

Push beyond your limits daily.

Working up to yesterday's limits is not the goal.

Pushing past those limits, making daily breakthroughs, is the goal.

Set out to make yesterday's maximum today's minimum.

And do the same thing tomorrow.

Remember, during wrestling practice, when your coach would always go past the preannounced time he said the leg lifts were going to last?

Remember how that felt?
Remember not thinking that you could hold out any longer?
But you did.

You reached a new mental pain limit.

Do that every day in every aspect of your life.

And see how your life expands.

RULE #27
BE THE GUY WHO SETS THE BAR

I believe in being strong
When everything seems
To be going wrong.
Audrey Hepburn

In every practice, there is always one wrestler who is convinced that they have reached their mental and physical limit.

They will look around for confirmation, to see if any of their teammates have also reached their limit.

To their amazement, their teammates will still be doing more, giving more, taking more pain.

After seeing this, the wrestler will suddenly un-convince themselves that they had reached their mental and physical limits and get back to work.

Suddenly they can do more.

They can go further.
They can absorb more pain.

On this day, the guy next to them set the bar.

On another day they will set the bar.

That is what being a teammate is all about.

****

At the NCAA's a few years back, Barry Davis, the
then head coach of the Wisconsin Badgers,
was asked how wrestling prepares a young man for
life, and he responded,

"Your phone is going to ring someday. It will.
And on the other end, you're going to hear
something that you don't like, but you must deal
with it.
When that phone rings, you can't run away.
You must answer it, and whatever it is, you must
deal with it.
The sport of wrestling facilitates that.
The sacrifices and sufferings in wrestling help
prepare young men for when that phone rings.
I believe that."
Undoubtedly, there will reach a time in your life,
after wrestling, when your new teammates, your
family, will face adversity and someone within your

family will be convinced that they can't go on anymore.

That they have reached their limit.

They have convinced themselves that they can't do anymore, give any more, or take any more pain.

They will look around for confirmation, to see if anyone else in the family is at their limit also.

Here is where the wrestler in you must take over.

Be the guy who sets the bar.

Decide not to be a product of your environment, commit to having your environment be a product of you.

When your family looks around for confirmation that you are also at your limit, they need to be amazed that you are not stopping.

You are doing more.

You are going further.

You are absorbing more pain.

Your actions will convince your family that they have more to give.

And they will give more.

Because they see you doing so.

And one day they will do so for you.

And that is what being a family is all about.

Rule #28
Anyone, Anytime, Anywhere

The three toughest fighters
I ever fought were
Sugar Ray Robinson,
Sugar Ray Robinson &
Sugar Ray Robinson.
I fought Sugar so many times,
I'm surprised I'm not diabetic.
Jake LaMotta

Mark West was an undefeated New York State Champion in his freshmen year in high school.

My son Travis was an undefeated New York State Champion in his senior year.

In their respective championship seasons,
Mark and Travis had a combined record of 94-0.

Before high school, as youth wrestlers,
Mark and Travis wrestled each other 14 times.

Mark won all 14 matches.

I believe it was those 14 consecutive losses to Mark as a youth wrestler that galvanized Travis into the wrestler he needed to become to be an undefeated New York State Championship.

I also believe, in a small way, it was Marks 14 consecutive wins over Travis that helped him become an undefeated State Champion as well.

Why do I believe this?

I believe Mark and Travis both benefitted from having the wrestling attitude of Anyone, Anytime, Anywhere.

Whenever Mark and Travis were scheduled to wrestle each other, they wrestled.

No matter when their matchup occurred,
no matter how often they wrestled,
no matter if they previously wrestled each other in the last tournament, or just wrestled yesterday,
or last week, or last month, they always wrestled.

And by doing so, they both got better; in different ways, but they both got better.

If Marks name was on one line of the bracket, and Travis's name was on the other, they wrestled.

Here is the cycle from which both wrestlers benefitted.

Travis and Mark would wrestle.

Mark would win.

Travis and I would review the video and figure out what made Mark win the match. We studied how Mark scored his points and where he may be vulnerable.

We would then go into practice that week with a focus and concentration to learn how to stop Marks attack and how to counter his moves.

Travis practiced with a purpose; to clean up the areas where Mark had exposed him.

Soon after, Travis and Mark would wrestle again, with Travis feeling as prepared as ever to compete against Mark because of the work he put in after his last loss to Mark.

Mark would find a new way to beating Travis, with new moves, and a different attack then the ones we had prepared for.

After the loss, Travis and I would immediately review the video to see how Mark won, dissecting his new attack and coming up with a plan to counter his latest attack.

Once again, we would go into practice that week and diligently work on stopping Marks new attack and countering his newly incorporated moves.

Travis and Mark would wrestle again, and once again Travis would go into the match feeling prepared, after eliminating his newfound flaw.

Mark, once again knowing we were going to go back to the video to study him came up with a new way of beating Travis, with new moves and another attack.

This cycle repeated itself for fourteen matches.

When it was all said and done, Travis wrestling Mark 14x wound up being the most valuable thing Travis had done as a youth wrestler.

And I believe it was also one of the most valuable things Mark did as well.

Mark found 14 ways to beat a quality wrestler.

Travis corrected 14 ways a quality wrestler beat him.

That is the power of anyone, anytime, anywhere.

I give both Mark and Travis a lot of credit.

Never once did Mark say,
"I don't want to wrestle Travis. Heck, I've beaten him 14x already."

No, every time Travis stepped foot on the mat, Mark beat him.

Never once did Travis ever say,
"Let's not go to that tournament. I'm just going to have to wrestle Mark again."

No, Travis went to the next tournament seeking to wrestle Mark again.

No matter how often, no matter what length of time there was between each match, no matter how mundane it became for Mark to beat Travis, no matter if losing one time to Travis would have been devastating enough to supersede all his wins against him, Mark kept wrestling and kept finding a new way of winning.

The process of this cycle was invaluable to both wrestlers.

It made Travis better as each time he wrestled Mark a new flaw in his game was found, which he then went back and corrected.

After 14 cycles, Travis was nearly flawless.

I also believe the cycle made Mark a better wrestler as he learned 14 ways to beat a quality wrestler, never relying on any one way to win.

I tell this story because I believe there is great value in it.

So often, nowadays you see guys who are afraid to face the same wrestler multiple times for fear that the other wrestler might "figure them out."

Shame on them if they can be "figured out" so easily.

In fourteen matches, Mark couldn't be "figured out" because he did the work to stay one step ahead.

He grew.

He trained to find a new way to win.

And he did.

I have seen elite wrestlers forfeit a semi-final match in a major tournament during the regular season so that they wouldn't face their expected postseason rival anywhere other than in the state final.

Shame on him to think he could only beat his opponent one time.

So often, nowadays you see guys who won't wrestle the same opponent in a short period of time, because their flawed thinking is,
"I can only beat him once, and I'd rather save that win for the right time."

So often nowadays you see guys relying on the same moves to win, never expanding their repertoire; thus, it is only a matter of time before their opponents were able to figure them out.

So often nowadays wrestlers are afraid to lose to someone they have beaten multiple times as they fear that the one-loss would loom larger than all their combined wins against that same opponent.

When one allows fear to steer a crash is imminent.

So often nowadays wrestlers try to pick and choose the spots where they perform to preserve an artificial ranking of being ranked #1 instead of wrestling the best competition available.

I believe by wrestling Anyone, Anytime, Anywhere, allows you to reach an unbridled level of excellence.

RULE #29
IMPOSE YOUR WILL

If you haven't the strength
To impose your own terms upon life,
Then you must accept the terms it offers you.
T.S. Eliot

Good things do not just happen in life.

You need to make them happen.

Taking massive, immediate action, makes good things happen.

Even after taking massive, immediate action, your efforts will run into resistance.

To overcome resistance requires grit.

To do what you set out to do will require more attempts than you had planned.

During these multiple attempts, doubt will start to creep in.

Purpose will allow you to persevere through doubt.

As purpose trumps doubt.

To persevere with purpose requires will.

Will is the process of converting what you want into reality for your unique reasons.

That is where mental toughness comes in.

Iowa University head wrestling coach, Tom Brands once said,

"Finding solutions to difficult situations, solutions to places where you are not comfortable going; That all comes down to work ethic, mental toughness, and attitude."

Ralph Waldo Emerson eloquently said, "What lies behind us, and what lies before us, are tiny matters compared to what lies within us."

Your will is what lies within you.

It is your why.

Use your why to impose your will.

Rule #30
Never Bet Against an Underdog Who Has The Heart of a Champion

If there is a Goliath infront of you,
That means there's a David inside of you.

It happens at every weigh-in at every wrestling event, by almost every wrestler in the country.

The "sizing up your opponent," as he steps on the scale ritual.

Then, predetermining the outcome of the match based on the recent visual of your opponents' muscularity and physique.

There is no doubt that strength is a vital ingredient to success in wrestling.

But strength can be measured in different ways.

Strength does not only come from one's physique or muscles; it can also come from one's heart.

And one's heart cannot be seen by stepping on the scale at a weigh-in.

It is only visible during battle.

What most people neglect to factor in when viewing a physical specimen stepping on the scale is that to partake in a battle requires effort.

And effort makes your body release lactic acid.

And lactic acid is the kryptonite to muscles; it makes them slow and lethargic.

What those same people also neglected to factor into the equation is that winning a battle requires having a purpose.

And when one has a purpose, "heart" is released during battle which makes even the smallest muscles and the tiniest physique more powerful than one could imagine or foresee.

If you want a truer indication of your opponent, don't size up his biceps when he is on the scale, observe his heart as it responds to battle.

RULE #31
PRIORITIZE OR AGONIZE

Many of us never realize our greatness
Because we get sidetracked
By secondary activity.
Og Mandino

A Wrestling Life.
An Academic Life.
A Social Life.

As a wrestler, you get to choose 2 of the 3.

You can choose any 2, but never 3.

I repeat you can choose any 2, but never 3.

If you are arrogant enough to attempt to choose all 3, the choice you value the most will suffer the greatest.

Test it at your own peril.

There is not enough time, nor do you have enough energy to accomplish everything every day.

There will be days you will have to sacrifice something you value.

When you live in order with your priorities and then run out of time or energy in your day, the choice of least value to you will get sacrificed.

When you live out of order of your priorities, what gets sacrificed is of the choice of most value to you.

To achieve the life you envision, you must live each day in order and harmony with your priorities.

As an adult, there will be three new choices.

A Healthy Life.
A Family Life.
An Undisciplined Life.

You get to choose 2 of the 3.

You can choose any 2, but never 3.

I repeat you can choose any 2, but never 3.

If you are arrogant enough to attempt to choose all 3 the one you value the most will suffer the greatest.

Test it at your own peril.

Living life in order and harmony of your priorities sometimes will seem boring, like you are missing out on something.

You are.

You will be missing out on dealing with the agony of regret and missing out on cleaning up the messes of an undisciplined life.

Prioritize or agonize.

A wrestler knows the reward is always correlated to the exact degree of difficulty of the task.

RULE #32
ALWAYS CHOOSE THE HARDER OPTION

Once you get past the point
Of expecting life to be easy,
It becomes much less difficult.

I can always tell a wrestler out in the real world.

They seem to always gravitate toward the difficult.

When given a choice, a normal person will choose the path of least resistance.

When a wrestler is given a choice, they will always choose the path of difficulty.

Why is that?

Because wrestlers know that nothing ever worth it was easy to obtain, and that nothing easy to obtain was ever worth it.

A wrestler knows the reward is always correlated to the exact degree of difficulty of the task.
And that choosing the harder option will separate you from the crowd in any endeavor.

That is why wrestlers always choose the harder option.

Life is the same way.
Most people in life will choose the option that requires the least amount of effort for a smaller short-term result.

Choosing the harder option, which sacrifices obtaining a small short-term result for a more enduring long term reward will require more time and effort.

Hard work works.

In a weird perverse way, wrestlers have been trained to understand that in the long run,
the harder option is always the better option.

I've never heard a wrestler say,
"Let's go easy in practice today."

Wrestlers always choose the harder option.

And in the long run, they are rewarded for doing so.

RULE #33
WEIGH EVERYTHING

The price of anything
Is the amount of life you exchange for it.
Henry David Thoreau

Have you ever witnessed a wrestler weigh his food?

Why do you think they do that?

Wrestlers weigh their food because they understand
the Universal law of cause and effect.

A person can do whatever they choose,
but there will always be a price to pay for one's
actions.

If you are willing to pay the price, do the action.

If you are unwilling to pay the price, don't.

Can you eat mashed potatoes when you are two
pounds over?

You can; you always have a choice.

But by doing so will require you to run an extra mile on top of the already grueling schedule you have planned to lose the two pounds you already need to lose.

Not worth it.

Can you eat 16 ounces of chicken the night before weigh-in while being on weight?

Yes, worth it.

Clean protein can be floated off overnight.

Want to eat a burger instead?

Need to run a mile.

Most people mistakenly look at a wrestler who weighs his food and says he isn't allowed to eat.

That is not true.

A wrestler weighs his food to determine if the price he must pay for eating is something he is willing to pay.

If the food a wrestler weighs has dense nutritional value, the answer will be yes, it is worth it.

If it is of low nutritional value, then no, it won't be worth the price.

Life is the same way.

You can do anything that you want in life.

Everything will have a cost.

Weigh every one of your decisions carefully.

And decide ahead of time if you are willing to pay the price.

If you do something stupid; your choice.

Remember, you're going to have to pay a larger price than just running a mile.

Look at your life as always being on weight.

If the action you want to do will improve the quality of your life or the life of a loved one, the answer will be yes; it will be worth the cost.

If the action you want to do will not improve the quality of your life or the life of a loved one, then the answer will be no, it will not be worth the price you have to pay.

Weigh every action, every decision, every choice in life, and always remember how grueling it was trying to get those mashed potatoes off an hour before weigh-in.

Rule #34
Delay Gratification

For everything you have missed,
You have gained something else,
And for everything you gain,
You lose something else.

We live in a microwave society.

Everyone wants instant gratification, instant success.

The problem is that success doesn't come in an instant formula.

Success requires years of hard work, sacrifice, and perseverance.

Understand, for every gratification you delay,
you will receive an even bigger reward tomorrow.

Be strong enough to resist the temptation of an immediate reward to put yourself in position to receive a greater, more enduring reward in the future.

No seed planted today is ever harvested today.

Every hour invested in delaying gratification nurtures a seed which will be more bountifully sown tomorrow.

Rule #35
Always Move Forward

Success is not final.
Failure is not fatal.
It is the courage to continue that counts.
Winston Churchill

An unrelenting forward attack.

Never backing up.

Never stopping.

Moving forward for seven minutes.

Leaving everything you have out on the mat.

That's the Iowa Style.

Approach life the same way.

An unrelenting pursuit of becoming the best version of yourself.

Never backing up.

Never stopping.

Failing forward.

Putting everything you got into each new day.

Having an unrelenting quest for a better life.

To improve the quality of life for yourself and others.

RULE #36
YOU WIN
OR YOU LEARN

If we shall be quiet
And ready enough,
We will find compensation
In every disappointment.
Henry David Thoreau

You win, or you learn.

When you adjust your thinking that a loss is not a loss, but rather it is a learn, then both the win and the loss will prove to be beneficial to your success.

When you incorporate "You win, or you learn," you will always win because in both cases you come out ahead.

Tom Brands said,

"When things don't go the way that you want them to go, get the next best thing."

When your goal is to win, and you don't, the next best thing is to learn why.

Expect, then inspect, then apply.

RULE #37
TAKE COMPLETE AND ABSOLUTE OWNERSHIP

I am the master of my fate.
I am the captain of my soul.
William Ernest Henley
Invictus

Placing blame or making excuses is a futile endeavor.

It wastes time and energy.

I have never seen a wrestler who came off the mat placing blame or making an excuse ever wrestle his next match with a better outcome.

Blame and excuses lead to a downward spiral because subconsciously you are telling yourself that they were out of your control; thus, cannot be fixed.

Downward spirals are not conducive to winning championships.

By taking complete and absolute ownership to all circumstances, you are telling your subconscious mind that you are in control and can fix what needs to be fixed to have a better outcome next time.

This action leads to improved performance.

Improved performance leads to championships.

****

In life, there will be many opportunities to blame others for poor performance.

There will be many opportunities to make an excuse as to why something bad occurred.

Don't.

Always remember that your objective is for better future performance.

Take complete and absolute ownership instead. Doing so will give you the greatest opportunity for future success.

Remember, you are the master of your fate; you are the captain of your soul.

Rule #38
Don't Make The Same Mistake Twice

Once is a mistake.
Twice is a choice.

There are too many mistakes in this world to make once.

Don't exponentially increase the number of mistakes there are available to make by repeating one.

Mistakes can be very useful.

When you make a mistake and learn from it,
that mistake is not as a waste.

When you make a mistake, and you do not learn from it, well, that is a waste of time and energy which are both in limited supply in life.

Don't waste either by not applying a lesson that you have already paid the price to learn.

Take complete responsibility for your actions and ownership for their results.

RULE #39
BLAME IS A LOSERS GAME

If you would like to destroy, blame.
If you would like to ignite, praise.
If you would like to wound, yell.
If you would like to heal, listen.
If you want to fix, take responsibility.

If you don't like what happened, don't blame, adjust.

When you adjust you correct the mistake.

When you blame, you keep yourself trapped in the mistake.

Losers stay trapped.

Winners escape the mistake by adjusting.

Remember when you point the finger at someone else, three will be pointing back at you.

Take complete responsibility for your actions and ownership for their results.

We have all put everything into this sport, and then suddenly it doesn't work out, and it just breaks your heart.

RULE #40
FIGURE IT OUT

To struggle and to understand.
Never the last without the first.
George Mallory

We have all been in that hallway before.

We have all lost that tough match.

We have all put everything into this sport,
and then suddenly it doesn't work out, and it just
breaks your heart.

What do we do?

What does a wrestler do?

They don't quit.

They don't stop.

They get back to work.

They work harder.

They throw themselves deeper into the sport.

They figure it out.

They revise their plan.

That is exactly what wrestling is about.

That is exactly what life is about.

Whenever you face a situation in life where you find yourself in that proverbial hallway, don't feel sorry for yourself.

Don't quit.

Don't stop.

Get back to work.

Work harder.

Figure it out.

RULE #41
TRUST YOURSELF

Intuition is
Seeing with the soul.
Dean Koontz

Your intuition is a key component in figuring it out.

People get similar results because they act and respond similarly.

Trust your instincts when they scream out to you to act differently.

Sometimes it takes making a wrong turn that requires you to make another wrong turn that somehow puts you back on course.

You can never see the two wrong turns turning into the right path ahead of time.

But your intuition can.

It can see around corners and over mountains.

It can see two wrong turns ahead.

Be still and listen to your soul.

It will whisper to you.

Trust it.

Trust it even when it is telling you to do something that is not completely solving the problem.

As it may be working a few steps ahead.

RULE #42
MAKE ADJUSTMENTS
NOT EXCUSES

There will always be rocks in the road ahead of us.
They will be stumbling blocks or stepping-stones.
It all depends on how you use them.
Friedrich Nietzsche

Excuses provide a reason why something didn't happen in the past without an adjustment to correct the reason to why it won't happen again in the future.

It is the adjustment that is key, so that same thing will not happen again in the future.

Adjustments take the reason and add an action that solves the problem.

Always go further than looking for the reason why something didn't work out as you had liked.

Invest the time to look for the adjustment you need to make to ensure it won't happen again in the future.

You win, or you learn.

Apply what you learned when you didn't win and then that non-win can never be deemed a loss.

RULE #43
DEEP IN THE DIFFICULT
YOU WILL FIND
THE BEST VERSION OF YOURSELF

The gem cannot be polished without friction,
Nor man perfected without trials.
Rumi

Feel blessed when faced with difficulty.

As difficulty is the sculptor of men.

One of the greatest, most profound realizations I have ever had in my life was the understanding that all adversity that I ever faced in my life was designed to bring out the best in me, to turn me into the best version of myself.

Since then, I have always been up for the challenge of the transformation.

When I am deep in difficulty, I feel blessed knowing a better version of me is in the process of being sculpted.

I imagine the Universe during the sculpting, with a chisel in its hand and Michelangelo's quote hanging on its wall,

"Every block of stone has a statue inside it, and it is up to the sculptor to discover it," while sending more adversity my way.

I truly believe that life doesn't happen to me;

It happens for me.

In her book, "Death and Dying," Elisabeth Kubler-Ross wrote,

"The most beautiful people we have known are those who have known defeat, known suffering, known struggle, known loss, and have found their way out of the depths.

These persons have an appreciation, a sensitivity, and an understanding of life that fills them with compassion, gentleness, and deep loving concern.

Beautiful people do not just happen."

Rule #44
You've Got to Love
The Taste of Blood

Everyone has a plan
Until they get punched in the mouth.
Mike Tyson

Wrestling is hard.

It's one on one verse a highly trained, highly skilled, highly motivated opponent.

Sometimes that opponent is going to get the best of you.

When that occurs, the best of you needs to come out.

They say a wrestling match doesn't start until you're tired.

I say the fight doesn't start until you get punched in the mouth.

The best wrestlers love to fight.

It is when the true competitor inside them comes out.

Life is hard.

It is a battle, a fight.

Sometimes life will get the best of you.

When it does, the best of you must come out.

When life punches you in the mouth, wipe your lip and let that punch bring out the best of you.

Let it ignite the fight in you.

Imagine you were just thrown out of bounds by your rival and the whole crowd just gasped in awe.

Now come back and give life that beating, just like you would do if you got thrown out of bounds during a competitive wrestling match by a rival.

RULE #45
FIND A WAY

A voice calls from within to go on.
And so, he goes on.
When asked why he did not quit
John Steven Aquari responded,
My country didn't send me 5,000, miles to start a
race.
They sent me 5,000 miles to finish the race.
John Stephan Ahkwari
Last Place Finisher
Marathon Runner from Tanzania
1968 Mexico City Olympics

I train a few wrestlers each year, mostly mental
training for peak performance.

Before I start to train any wrestler, I always ask them
why they wrestle?

Why do they want to win?

Why does it mean so much to them?

Why do I do that?

Because I understand during their journey to greatness, they will be tested.

They will be required to do things that seem out of whack, unfair, and without payoff.

And there will come a time when they will question whether all the work, sacrifice, and discipline are worth it.

And I need to know why enduring extreme pain is worth it to them.

Each of us has a special reason, a why, a driving force as to why we are willing to endure so much un-comfortability for so little pleasure.

Where does ones why come from?

It comes from within.

When you feel that you are part of something bigger, when you are doing this for more than yourself, then your why will be greater than any obstacle, and you will endure.

Out of all the rules you learn on the mat, this is going to be one of the most useful off the mat.

Some things defy logic.

Some things defy the odds.

Some things are inborn where you just know.

Those are the things you need to make happen.

How?

You find a way.

No matter what.

Whatever it takes.

Somehow.

Anyhow.

You figure it out.

If your why is strong enough, you will endure.

I don't condone sucking weight, but I do believe that everyone should experience it at least once.

It will help one understand what it means to have to be at your best when you feel your worst.

Rule #46
Be at Your Best
When You Feel Your Worst

The flower that blooms in adversity
Is the rarest and most beautiful of all.
Walt Disney

I don't condone sucking weight, but I do believe that everyone should experience it at least once.

It will help one understand what it means to have to be at your best when you feel your worst.

We have all been there.

Not eating or drinking for a long period,
being dangerously near dehydration with all your energy zapped from you and then having to take the mat against an opponent who not only wants to defeat you but also wants to humiliate you in the process.

No food, no water, no recovery time, no energy.

Regardless, peak performance is still expected.

Against an elite opponent.

With your season at stake.

And everything you have worked for in complete jeopardy.

Experiencing cutting weight in wrestling prepares you to be at your best when you feel your worst in life.

There is no other endeavor on earth that will mimic how it feels to be a parent of a sick child.

As an adult, there will be a night where you will have to stay up with your sick child, and then you will be required to go to work the next day and perform at your best with your job on the line.

And then repeat the process the next day.

And the next.

And the next.

With no recovery time, and no energy.

And peak performance in every aspect of your life will still be expected.

It has been said that a wrestling match starts once you become tired.

Everyone can wrestle with good technique and good discipline when the conditions are right.

Everyone is full of hope when they are winning.

But only the few can prosper when the conditions are grueling.

When you are behind in the score.

When things look bleak.

When life and circumstance seem unfair, unjust.

The key to doing so is to be able to perform at your best when you feel your worst.

To keep your belief.

Your discipline.

Your hope.

In life, when things are going wrong, and you feel your worst is when your family will rely on you the most.

You must come through.

When you are in this situation, when you feel your worst and must perform your best, just get through the weight cut.

Make the weight.

And then perform your best.

You've done this many time before.

RULE #47
BE ABLE TO DO MORE
WITH LESS

Cover the eyes to hear.
Cover the ears to see.
Austin Kleon

Wrestlers are trained to have high energy on low calories.

They sweat without having an intake of water.

They train all week, then perform to an empty crowd.

They get their hand raised to very little applause.

They learn to harness their energy, their focus, and desire.

They are resourceful in everything they do.

They maximize their time, energy, and performance.

There is no waste.

They learn to do more with less.

****

Everyone has different circumstances in life.

Some have plenty of opportunities, and others only a few.

Some have many resources; others have limited resources.

Some have much luck, and others have no luck at all.

In life, don't fret over the number of opportunities, resources, and luck you have, you've been trained to make the most out of whatever you have.

What you have is enough.

Don't waste your time wishing, hoping for more opportunities, resources, or luck.

Do what you have always done.

Invest your time into using what you have to its fullest capability.

Do more with less.

There is something inside the over-matched wrestler that is unwilling to listen to the voice which will lead him to defeat.

Rule #48
Be Unwilling To Quit

There is nothing like the sight
Of an amputated spirit.
There's no prosthetic for that.
Lieutenant Colonel Frank Slade
The Scent of a Woman

If you watch closely, you can see it happen in
every wrestling tournament.

A match where one wrestler fights and another
decides to quit.

A match between two evenly matched
wrestlers where one wrestler breaks the others will.

A match where one wrestler convinces his opponent
that he will not win, and his opponent believes him,
and he stops trying.

An experienced eye can pick up the exact moment
when it happens.

It may happen after one wrestler gets shut down
after a relentless offensive pursuit.

Or gives up points on the line, or on a cheap tilt or allows his opponent to score with short time or come out on the wrong side of an extraordinary scramble, or he lets a bad call affect his focus and his mental state.

Whenever and however it happens, the shift in the effort by one wrestler is dramatic.

A once-tight score suddenly gets blown open.

A wrestler who was once defending all his opponent's shots at length, suddenly, can no longer defend any of the same shots he so valiantly defended just a minute earlier.

The crowd which formed to see the marquee matchup between two elite wrestlers disperses disappointed, as they came to see a superior effort, not resignation.

What happened?

Why is one wrestler now putting on a takedown clinic verse the other?

Did suddenly one wrestler lose all his talents?

Did suddenly one wrestler lose all his training?

Did suddenly one wrestler lose all his experience?

No, in the blink of an eye, one wrestler lost all his will.

The wrestler who quit let circumstances convince him that he could not win.

When a wrestler reaches this mental point, there may be time left on the clock, but the match is over.

There is no more try.

As try has been traded for resignation.

He is resigned to the fact that he will not win.

With try still left in the tank, he has predetermined his fate.

He is being let up and taken down at will.

It gets so bad that his opponent is attempting to let him up once more, only for the resigned wrestler to stay down and not turn and face him because he knows what is coming.

Another takedown.

He is resigned to stay down, to not attempt.

His goal has changed from winning the match to having the match end.

The one wrestler has convinced himself that resigning is less painful than trying.

****

In every tournament, one can also find a match where one wrestler, no matter the circumstances, is unwilling to quit.

It usually goes like this.

A wrestler is facing an opponent in which he is overmatched.

Few people are watching the match.

The overmatched wrestler gets thrown to his back.

He fights off his back for the whole first period only to be immediately put to his back again in the 2nd period; to fight some more.

While on his back fighting for his survival, he hears the few people watching the match whisper, "It's over."

He continues to fight anyway.

Every time the overmatched wrestler's shoulder blades get near the mat, he somehow miraculously surges them, to stay alive, even though the likelihood of a comeback is remote.

That doesn't matter to him.

What matters more to this over-matched wrestler is that he is forever unwilling to quit.

He is unwilling to surrender his will.

He is unwilling to listen to the wrong voices instructing him to take the path of least resistance, to resign and relax for just a second.

Which would end the match.

Instead, he continues to fight through the pain.

He is unwilling to be defeated for lack of try.

After spending two periods on his back,
the over-matched wrestler faces a third period.

He has the choice between top, bottom, and neutral.

He evaluates his options and realizes there is not one
option where he foresees a favorable outcome.

The realization doesn't faze him.

He chooses the top position.

He is immediately reversed and put on his back.

He has just fought off his back for the last four
minutes and now faces two more grueling minutes
having to do the same.

The rational thought would say it would be easier to
ease up for a fraction of a second and allow his
shoulder blades to graze the mat ever so slightly, for
a fall.

It would all be over then.

No one would blame him; he was over-matched.

But there is something inside the over-matched
wrestler that is unwilling to listen to rationale.

He is unwilling to listen to the voice which will lead
him to defeat.

He survives the first minute of the third period,
his fifth minute on his back.

It took every ounce of energy he had, to survive.

Just to face more pain.

His chance of winning the match has gone from
improbable to near impossible.

It would be very easy for him to end it all;
all he would have to do is collapse his shoulders,
and the match would be over.

But something inside of him can't.

Something inside of him is unwilling.

From his back, he glances up and sees two things; a crowd is forming around his mat, and the clock says that he has another minute left to fight.

He is out of energy.

He is beyond believing he will win the match.

He feels his shoulders nearing the mat; they are as close to the mat as they have been all match.

He is determined to keep his shoulders above the mat.

Somehow, he reaches down and taps into a reservoir of strength he never knew existed.

He is unwilling to allow his hard work to go for naught.

The ever-increasing crowd takes notice of his effort and starts to root for him not to get pinned.

They start counting down the seconds left in the match.

10, 9, 8…

3, 2, 1,

0.

A loud ovation erupts from the crowd.

The wrestler who has spent the last six minutes on his back untangles himself from his opponent and heads back to the circle.

The crowd is on their feet, applauding.

Not for the victor.

But for him.

For his effort.

For his refusal to allow circumstances to dictate his effort.

They realize they have just witnessed the essence of the sport.

The referee raises his opponent's hand as he storms
off the mat as if he has lost the match,
disgruntled because he didn't get the pin.
The over-matched wrestler who fought off his back
for six minutes is embraced by his teammates and
his coaches.

They swarm him as if he had won the match.

Because he has.

His will made him fight.

His will made him survive.

His will made him unwilling.

Unwilling to give in.

Unwilling to take the path of least resistance.

Unwilling to be broken.

Unwilling to quit.

RULE #49
BE UNBREAKABLE

He who has a why to live for
Can bear almost any how.
Fredrich Nietzsche

What makes one wrestler fight and another wrestler give up?

Is it talent?

It is not talent; it is something much more reliable than talent.

Is it training?

It is not training; it is something much more valuable than training.

Is it experience?

It is not experience; it is something much more invisible than experience.

It is will.

And it can't be taught, only discovered.

When one is willing to fight, fear is destroyed.

As fear is afraid of fight.

****

Wrestling is life.

There are times in life where circumstances will be presented to you, and you will have a decision to make.

Will you break and predetermine that you are unable to win, and become resigned not to try?

Or will you be unbreakable and unwilling to quit?

Which wrestler do you want to be?

Do you want to be the wrestler who still had try left in his tank but quit?

Or the overmatched wrestler who used up all his try, and didn't?

I was once told that the type of wrestler I was would be the kind of man I will be.

There was never a truer statement ever spoken to me in my life.

There is nothing more valuable to a wrestler than the realization that he is unbreakable.

There is nothing more valuable to a human in times of adversity than the realization that he is unbreakable.

That no matter the circumstances, he will survive.

How?

I don't know.

Just have the mindset,

"I've handled everything up until this point, and I will handle everything that comes my way in the future."

This realization allows one to not waste any time on worry, which provides no solutions, but instead to have peace of mind and live by intuition.

Be unbreakable.

It will all work out in the end.

If it hasn't yet worked out,

It is not the end.

Rule #50
Put Your Toe on the Line
And You Fight Like Hell

I know of no better life purpose
Than to perish
In attempting the great and impossible.
Friedrich Nietzsche

My first varsity wrestling match was against one of
the strongest wrestlers I ever knew.

I remember saying those exact words as I walked off
the mat at Commack South High School after
wrestling Adam Pitt in 1979.

Now, 40 years later, I am convinced that was one of
the truest statements I had ever made in my life.

If the disciplines of wrestling are designed to
convert high school wrestlers to men, to teach them
how to fight whatever life will throw at them, then
wrestling worked its wonders on Adam Pitt.

After a long struggle and fight against an opponent
much bigger than he, Adam passed away in 2018.

Before he passed, I had the pleasure of reconnecting with Adam after 38 years.

He contacted me after reading my book, "6 Minutes Wrestling with Life."

We messaged back and forth a few times.

At the time, I had no idea he was sick.

Until, I did what everyone in this generation does – check out one's Facebook page.

And there I saw post after post how Adam, through the way he lived his life, especially through his fight, had touched so many lives.

One post instantly struck me.

When asked how he dealt with his sickness each day, he said,

"You put your toe on the line, and you fight like hell."

Towards the end, our messages turned into phone calls, as Adam would call me on occasion.

During those phone calls, not many words were said, as talking was a struggle for him at this time, but that wasn't to say nothing was communicated – it was if he was transferring spirit to me instead.

It's amazing, but the silence on the phone had an immediate and amazing impact on me.

It wasn't awkward; it was the type of time you know is important when it's happening.

After every phone call with Adam, I felt renewed, energized.

And virtually nothing was said.

Nothing had to be said.

At the time Adam and I were both fighting a battle against an opponent much bigger and stronger than both of us – and we both knew it.

The days after talking with Adam when I felt I had had enough and the fight in me started to erode, I always referred to the silent phone calls we shared and the message he conveyed,

"You put your toe on the line, and you fight like hell."

That's all you can do.

And in the process, no matter what the outcome may be, people will see the fight and struggle and their spirits will be lifted, their approach will be changed, and their lives will be improved.

When you wrestle an opponent much bigger than you, you can win in ways other than scoring more points than them.

There is something about giving all you got and fighting no matter what, for as long as you can.

Even if the struggle ends in sorrow, sorrow transfers to spirit.

And spirit lasts forever.

RULE #51
BE THE FIRST ONE
BACK TO THE CIRCLE

The only pace
Is a suicide pace.
And today is a good day to die.
Steve Prefontaine

There is a split-second to decide.

You have just given every ounce of energy you had to win your match.

The buzzer just rang, and it's asking for more.

The match is tied.

You sit there on one knee in disbelief, contemplating how in the world after giving everything you had that the score can be tied.

It is at that moment when the clock starts ticking.

Before the very first tick, the next tick, you must decide.

Do you stop for a moment, admit being tired and doubt that you can go on?

Or do you take massive immediate action knowing you have more to give even after given everything you had?

The fight is asking for more.

The split-second decision you are about to make will dictate your fate.

I've seen it a million times, when the final whistle blows and both wrestlers sit there spent after given their all, the first wrestler back to the circle will ultimately win the match.

Always remember your mindset will always take you further than your body wants to go.

When you have given everything, and you don't know if there is anything left to give, remember your why and more will appear.

Show your opponent that you are ready, willing, and able to do everything to win.

That you will never be broken and that you will fight forever.

That the pace he is going to need to beat you is a pace that he doesn't have.

Decide early on to always be the first person back to the circle.

You always have more to give.

Just improve your position by doing the next right thing.

RULE #52
IMPROVE YOUR POSITION

Do what you can
With what you have
Where you are.
Teddy Roosevelt

Sometimes there reaches a point in a wrestling match where you realize you won't win the match.

You took too much risk and made too many mistakes.

Or perhaps you are just overpowered, overwhelmed or outmatched.

At that time, you will have two choices.

One is to quit and accept defeat, which I don't recommend.

If you do, you will not only lose the current battle, but you will also carry over a mental disadvantage with you to the battles yet to come.

Plus, like Denzel Washington points out,

"If you quit now, you'll end up right where you began.

And where you first began, you were desperate to be where you are right now."

The second option, the one I highly recommend is not to think too much, not worry about winning the match and concentrate on improving your position.

Ever so slightly.

Just build a base.

Get your feet underneath you and get back on your feet.

Granted, you may not be able to win this match, but improving your position will help you to start to win your future matches.

So, just improve your position.

Get off your belly and build a base.
Get your 1.

Put a few small wins together, and soon you will be back in the fight.

****

In life, there will be times when you will realize you are in an unwinnable situation.

You may have taken too much risk or made too many mistakes.

Or perhaps you are just overpowered, overwhelmed or outmatched.

When you find yourself in this situation,

Just build a base.

Just improve your position by doing the next right thing.

And repeat indefinitely, until you get your feet underneath you and you're able to fight again.

You can never go wrong by doing the next right thing.

RULE #53
SCORE THE NEXT 2 POINTS

The right choices and the wrong choices
You make at the moment
Will have little or no noticeable impact
On how your day goes for you.
Nor tomorrow, or the next day.
No applause, no cheers, no screams.
But it is those same undramatic,
Seemingly insignificant actions that,
When compounded over time
Will drastically affect how your life turns out.
Jeff Olson
The Slight Edge

Tom Ryan said it best,

"You are not always going to win.
We all know that a crowd will stand up if you fight
your heart out. If you are losing by 8 and you
somehow, someway, score the last takedown so you
lose by 6 and you save your team a point.

I've seen it.

I would expect that wrestler to fight that way if his wife were sick and needed help.

I would expect him to fight that way if something happened to his child.

I would expect him to fight that way in every situation in his life.

Those are the lessons that you must take away from the sport.

That I am on planet earth, and it may not be pretty, but nothing is going to stop me from fighting."

You can never go wrong by doing the next right thing.

Concentrate on what matters to the people that matter to you.

Fight for them always, especially when things are at their worst.

Just do the next right thing.

In wrestling, the next right thing is to score the next two points.

In life, the next right thing is to make the next right choice.

If not for you, then for the people you love.

Your payment will not always come in the normally expected fashion.

RULE #54
You Will Not Always
Get Paid For Your Work
Work Hard Anyway

No effort that we make
To attain the beautiful
Is ever lost.
Helen Keller

There will be times when you will do the work, and you won't get paid.

There will be times when you will do everything right, and things will still go wrong.

There will be times when you will put in a full season of training, and the payoff never happens.

What should you do when this happens?

Well, the best advice comes from Shakespeare when he wrote in Othello,

"The robbed that smiles steals something from the thief."

You see, some events are designed to discourage you.

To break you.

Don't let them.

Detach from negative emotions.

Flip the script and turn turmoil into fuel.

Be unable to be discouraged.

Believe you always get paid.

Even when you don't, you do.

Your payment will not always come in the normally expected fashion.

But hard work and a full effort always get paid.

Rule #55
Don't Let Defeat be Victorious

Sometimes losing the battle
Helps you find a way to win the war.

There is a difference between

Losing and being beaten.

Between resting and quitting.

Between having a setback and becoming
discouraged.

Between having failed and being a failure.

The difference is the former is used to fuel future
success, and the latter drains the fuel and ends your
dream.

In every loss, there is a learn.
In every rest, there is a restart.
In every setback, there is a comeback.
In every failed attempt, there is the winning
adjustment.

Use temporary defeat to fuel your future success.

RULE #56
BE INCAPABLE OF DISCOURAGEMENT

If we shall be quiet and ready enough,
We shall find compensation
In every disappointment.
Henry David Thoreau

It's going to take longer than you originally thought.

You are going to need to invest more effort than you ever would have liked to exert.

You are going to have to endure more pain than you planned.

Face more failed attempts than you thought would have been necessary.

Experience more setbacks than you rationally and logically should have ever had to go through.

There's going to be many times when your effort will not be rewarded, or even acknowledged.

Yes, at times it's going to suck.

For now.

You need to get through the suck.

Success always lags hard work.

When you have put in more effort than reward received, you must double down on belief, confidence, and enthusiasm.

You must continue to work yourself to the brink of collapse and tears.

You need to be able to do this indefinitely.

You need to have faith in the process.

For this part of the process is the final filtering system for creating greatness.

As your reward is not being unjustifiably held from you, it is being deferred for you.

Stored up, to be given to you in a lump sum, rather than in incremental pieces.

At this point in the process, what you do not do,
is more important than what you do.

To receive the reward of your hard work,

The reward you deserve,

The reward you have earned –

You need to be incapable of discouragement.

The path to success is lonely, uncomfortable, and dark, designed to make you quit and turn back.

Rule #57
You've Got to Get Through
The Suck

To be able to respond when it is time to get tough.
When you say to yourself,
"Man, I don't want to do this,"
But you know that you need to.
That is when you need to flip the switch
And just get through it.
Matt McDonough
Iowa Hawkeyes

The path to success is littered with unpleasantries.

Just ask Andy Dufresne who waded through a river
of human waste to swim to freedom in
"The Shawshank Redemption."

The path to success is lonely, uncomfortable, and
dark, designed to make you quit and turn back.

But like in a Spook Walk on Halloween the things
that jump out at you, designed to scare you to turn
around, when they are faced head-on with light,
they will recede and disappear.

To believe when all is well is not belief, it is good fortune.

RULE #58
ALWAYS BELIEVE

To believe in the things you can see and touch
Is no belief at all.
But to believe in the unseen
Is a triumph and a blessing.
Abraham Lincoln

Q: When is belief needed the most?

A: When circumstances are most dire.

When do people most lose belief?

When circumstances are most dire.

To believe when all is well is not belief,
it is good fortune.

To believe when all is nearly lost when logic would
tell you success is otherwise, is true belief.

Learn to doubt your doubt and believe in your
beliefs.

Especially when things are at their worst.

Tom Brands said,

"To have that kind of outlook, you have to have faith.

You must have something that you can attach yourself to that is outside.

Something that you know is extremely powerful, but you can't see."

Trust in your invisible, powerful, magical, force.

RULE #59
STAY THE COURSE

Still, 'round the corner, there may wait
A new road or a secret gate.
JRR Tolkien

You will beat 80% of the people by showing up, being disciplined, and dedicating your life to your mission.

You will beat up to 90% of the people by mastering the small details over years of hard work.

You will beat up to 98% of the people by staying the course.

The remaining 2% is going to be a dog fight.

The most determining factor of whether you will achieve your goals is your own will.

RULE #60
TRUST IN ONE THING
THE POWER OF YOUR OWN WILL

Always bear in mind
That your own resolution to succeed
Is more important than any one thing.
Abraham Lincoln

It is not the number of obstacles that will be in your path that will determine your success,
nor is it the degree of difficulty of the problems that lay ahead, nor is it the level of abundance of your resources to deal with those problems, no, the most determining factor of whether you will achieve your goals is your own will.

Will is defined as an internal predetermination of achievement despite the circumstances.

Will is more important than talent, resources, and opportunity.

It is more valuable than work ethic.

It is rarer than gold.

When you internally predetermine that you are going to accomplish something, you put the master at work.

You call on your subconscious mind to determine how.

To map out a path.

And soon after the Universe will start to help you.

Things will start breaking your way.

Every problem will have a clear solution.

Obstacles, chaos, and noise may delay you, but they won't stop you.

Your will is too powerful.

RULE #61
WHEN YOU CAN'T DO ANYMORE
YOU STILL HAVE MORE TO GIVE

Before you quit,
Try.
Ernest Hemingway

Do you remember doing leg lifts in practice?

I do.

"We're going to do ten one-minute leg raises, with 30 seconds rest in between sets," my high school coach would yell out at the end of practice.

The first eight sets would hurt, but I was able to do them without having to reach down.

But by the ninth set, my core would ache, my body would tremble, and time would stand still.

But somehow, I got through it.

After the ninth torturous set, my coach finally yelled, "Down."

The final 30 seconds of rest seemed non-existent.

"Up," my coach demanded for the last time.

"Hold 'em."

"Hold 'em," my coach would encourage us as he knew most of us were at our breaking points still with time remaining.

"30 seconds to go."

Half the room started to cheat by putting their hands under their hips for leverage.

The other half shimmied from side to side to transfer the pain,

"Hold 'em," my coach went on.

24 of the 30 wrestlers in the room dropped their legs down with a thump and a groan precisely at the one-minute mark. They didn't wait for coaches call of "Down," they were counting down every second remaining themselves.

"Hold 'em," my coach yelled out, ignoring the wrestlers who dropped their legs on their own at the 1-minute mark and concentrated on the remaining wrestlers willing to go past their mental boundaries.

"Hold 'em," he continued.

Another minute past.

"You got this," he encouraged.

Two more wrestlers had enough and dropped their legs.

Sweat exuded from my forehead as I clenched down with such intensity.

"Hold 'em; you can't drop now you've come this far."

Another two wrestlers ignored his advice and dropped their legs two minutes past the originally forecasted time.

They rolled over in pain and regret.

Now there are only two wrestlers left.

And I am one of them.

We are both well past our expectations to the pain of the torture of going past the promised time.

It is now 1 on 1.

"There is no way I am going to work this hard and then let someone beat me."

"There was no way I am going to suffer just to come in second," I say to myself in my mind.

I knew I'd never remember the suffering after I won, and I would always be acutely aware of it if I didn't.

There is no way I'm going to drop my legs now.

I've already suffered.

Now I want the prize.

At the 5-minute mark, I catch my 2nd wind.

I focus my mind and concentrate on a happy place.

Suddenly, I am lying on the beach, soaking in the sun.

I feel like I can go on forever.

That feeling lasts only a minute.

At the 6-minute mark, intense fatigue takes over.

I feel like I can't hold up my legs for another second.

I no longer can feel my lower extremities.

I am beyond pain.

I am numb to suffering.

I hear a thud.

Someone's legs have hit the ground, hard with a massive release.

I pray they weren't mine.

I unclench my eyes.

It wasn't me.

My legs are still a micro inch off the mat.

The other wrestler finally conceded, he elected to suffer and take 2nd place.

I refused to.

"You can drop your legs now," my coach yells out.

I catch my 3rd wind.

"If I've gone this far, I might as well go further," I answer.

"I've done all this work. There will never be another time that I will have this much work put in so I might as well see how far I can go."

Just a few seconds ago I didn't know if I could go on for another second, now suddenly, I have more to give.

So, I do.

****

They say when someone is stranded at sea
wandering in the middle of nowhere,
with no hope of rescue or energy left to survive even
one more second, that they get revitalized when land
off the horizon suddenly becomes visible to their
eye.

It doesn't matter that the land viewed off the
horizon is at the very least, eight miles away.

Eight miles is a significant distance.

It requires significant energy to swim eight miles.

It doesn't matter.

Now the mind is locked in on its targets.

Land is visible.

It's doable.

And with the resurgence of energy, of will, of
determination, rescue is believed to be within reach.

****

When you get to the point of feeling you can't do anymore, keep your eye open for land on the horizon.

You will have more to give.

Rule #62
Never Quit
Never
Means Not Ever

Never give in.
Never give in.
Never, never, never, never.
In nothing great or small,
Large or petty,
Never give in,
Except to convictions of honor and good sense.
Never yield to force.
Never yield to the apparently overwhelming might
Of the enemy.
Winston Churchill

Not Ever.

Inside the word NOT is the acronym OT, which stands for overtime.

Take out the OT and combine the N with Ever, and it creates the word Never.

Never quit.

Especially in overtime.

It takes a rare person to give everything, to only be told it wasn't enough and then have to reach down to find some more.

Logically, if this happens repeatedly, there must be an end to the well.

Energy is finite, right?

It may well be, but one's will isn't.

One's will *is* infinite.

Energy is replenished when one's will is tapped into.

****

The five most damaging words to accomplishment are,

"It's not worth it anymore."

Those five words have destroyed more dreams than failure.

They have stifled accomplishment, sabotaged more dreams, and produced more retirements for athletes than any others.

Those five words are dream killers, retirement makers, and success cappers.

"It's not worth it anymore,"

"The price is too high,"

"I don't want to pay the price."

That's what those five words confess to your soul.

Remember, the price will always be higher than we thought it would be.

It is always higher than it should be.

It is always higher than we had planned.

When you pay the price you felt should be enough and then realize it will not be enough, you have two choices.

Either, walk away and have all that you paid out go unfulfilled, or reach down and pay more, maybe even a lot more.

Quality things cost more.

Never give in.

Not Ever.

Never.

If it was worth it for you to begin, it is certainly most worth it for you to finish.

RULE #63
THERE IS AN OPEN CIRCLE

Every wall is a door.
Emerson

As a teenager, my goal and mission in life was to win a New York State High School Wrestling Championship.

I committed myself to a lifestyle, I made the sacrifices, I put in the time, I starved myself, shaved my head, I had the hunger, the desire, and the determination, but I came up short.

For many years after it seemed like I got nothing out of my six years of total dedication to the sport, that the trade-off of what I gave and what I got in return was way out of whack.

I hated wrestling for it.

To put every ounce of my soul into achieving something, and to get nothing out of it in return, was beyond my comprehension and unreconcilable to me.
I couldn't justify it in my head.

I felt this way for twenty-six years.

And then one-day adversity struck my life.

And slowly but surely, I started to realize just how much the sport of wrestling had given back to me.

Much more than I ever knew.

When life throws you to your back, you need to know how not to get pinned, get off your back, and do enough to make up the difference to win.

"There is an open circle."

This mantra is what my high school coaches would say to me during wrestling practice when they knew I was physically exhausted and was about to rest for a moment.

There was an open circle on the wrestling mat, and if I was interested, I could get out there and do more.

This mantra keeps ringing in my ears.
To achieve the results you want, you need to do the things others are not willing or able to do.

"There is an open circle."

Meaning there is still more that you could do.

Don't rest now; this is where the difference is made.

To work when you are mentally and physically exhausted gets you to the next level.

"There is an open circle."

When I heard those words back in high school, I would immediately ignore my fatigue and realize there was still more I could do.

"There is an open circle."

Today, when I reach the point of physical and mental exhaustion in my daily battle verse life, I silently say to myself,

"There is an open circle."

And my wrestling muscle memory kicks in, "There is no time for rest.

It is time to get back to work.

There is an open circle."

Rule #64
It Is Going to Take
More Than One Effort

You may have to fight a battle
More than once, to win it.
Margaret Thatcher

If you want to beat an average wrestler, shoot once.

If you want to beat an above average wrestler,
put two shots together.

If you want to beat an elite wrestler, you will need a
relentless offensive attack without hesitation.

Having a relentless offensive attack without
hesitation puts your opponent off balance,
unguarded, it wears down his defense where you
can then take advantage of his vulnerability.

The key to scoring is to get through your opponent's
defense.

One effort is easy for your opponent to defend.

It doesn't cause him to get too much out of position, and it allows him the time to reset and get back into a good defensive position before your next shot.

Two attempts will make your opponent more vulnerable on the second attempt, force him to have less balance.

And if the second attempt is made immediately, before he has a chance to reset, he will be unable to stop your attack.

Great wrestlers have quickness, great balance, and mobility.

Great wrestlers are quick enough, with enough balance and mobility to stop two shots in succession.

That is why they are great.

There reaches a point though, maybe 3, 4, 5 attempts in, where your relentless pursuit without hesitation will prove much for even an elite wrestler to defend.

Your relentless pursuit without hesitation will get them to be off-balance, fatigued, and vulnerable.

****

Life is the same way.

Many times in life, a person will have one attack in the pursuit of their goal.

Life has enough experience to stop one isolated attack.

Sometimes it is experienced enough to stop two continuous attempts.

In my experience, rarely is life skilled enough to stop a relentless pursuit of your goal without hesitation.

That's how you score in life.

With sustained multiple efforts, without hesitation.

By being relentless.

Talent + Work + Time + Grit
Equals Success

Rule #65
Natural Talent
Without Work, Time and Grit
Will Go Unfulfilled

Without effort
Your talent is nothing more than
Unmet potential.
Without effort
Your skill is nothing more than
What you could have done
But didn't.
Angela Duckworth
Grit

Natural Talent + Work + Time + Grit = Success

Natural talent is only one part of the formula for success.

Natural talent needs to be teamed up with work, time, and grit to be successful.

Natural Talent - Work - Time - Grit = Regret

Natural talent alone is inadequate for continued success.

As Herb Brooks said, "You do not have enough talent to win with talent alone."

By itself, natural talent will do more harm than good as one will tend to over-rely on such talent, which will make one extremely vulnerable.

When natural talent is teamed up with passion, a tenacious work effort, and mental toughness, it becomes part of an unbeatable winning formula.

There are no shortcuts to excellence.

Talent is only one part of the equation.

It is the most mishandled, dangerous part.

Reliance on natural talent alone is an attempt not to do the work necessary, not to put in the time required, and not to experience the pain that turns natural talent into skill.

The more naturally talented one is, the less one believes hard work has had as much to do with honing their craft as it has.

Talent needs grit to thrive long term.

Talent without grit will prove fruitless and go unfulfilled.

Grit is a combination of passion and perseverance.

It is toughness and tenacity tied together.

It is a high-level effort exerted over long periods.

The reverse is also true.

The less naturally talented you are, the more you rely on hard work to hone your craft.

In actuality, the real talent is the ability to put the hard work in over time and to grit it out during the hard times.

There will reach a point where the hard work, time, and grit can turn negligible natural talent into skill.

Skill soon surpasses natural talent because skill continues to get better while natural talent without hard work, time, and grit, withers.

Work ethic is often the naturally talented athletes Achilles Heel.

In Greek Mythology it was forecasted that Achilles would die young.

So, his mother took him down to the river Styx, which was thought to have magical powers of invulnerability.

She dipped him in the river holding him by his heel.

Achilles went on to become a warrior and survived many battles.

Achilles' life seemed invulnerable.

Until he died when a poisonous arrow hit him in his only vulnerable place.

His heel.

There is not an athlete alive that has been completely dipped in the river of invincibility.

Every athlete has a vulnerability.

Never over-rely solely on your natural talent,
or you will take a potential asset and make it your vulnerability; your Achilles Heel.

Remember behind every champion is a combination of natural talent, acquired skill, passion, hard work, and perseverance.

Success is never easy.

Even when it seems like it comes naturally for some, don't be fooled.

If you peeled back the layers to their success, you would find a whole lot of grit there as well.

As Angela Duckworth said,
"Nobody wants to show you the hours and hours of becoming. They'd rather show the highlight of what they become."

Without hard work, time, and grit, natural talent will go unfulfilled.

Rule #66
Don't Let One Loss
Beat You Twice

Pay attention
To what you pay attention to.
Amy Krause Rosenthal

Have you ever witnessed a wrestling semi-slide?

Or perhaps experienced one yourself?

It is one of the most helpless experiences to witness.

Walt Whitman wrote,

"Battles are lost in the same spirit in which they are won."

There has never been a truer statement written regarding the wrestling semi-slide.

A wrestling semi-slide is when a wrestler experiences a traumatic loss in the semi-finals, and instead of reconciling the loss, they fixate on it.

Their mental focus shifts from their goal to their loss.

They are no longer present in the present; they are fixated on the past.

Instead of resetting a new goal, because their original goal is now unobtainable, they refuse to, and they persistently attempt to get back something that they can't.

And their mind gets stuck in an endless, infinite loop, trying to solve an unsolvable problem.

This fixation on the loss makes them unable to recover quick enough for their next match which they lose to an inferior opponent.

Their self-sabotage repeats itself the following match too, against an even more inferior opponent.

Thus, completing the slide from the semi-finals, all the way down to 8th place.

Allowing one loss to beat them twice.

The wrestling semi-slide is a torturous experience for all involved.

Like every coach, parent or any other person who has ever attempted to shake some sense into the wrestler during a semi-slide knows, witnessing a semi-slide is one of the most helpless feelings one could ever experience in the sport.

No matter what you say, no matter what you do, no matter if you use fear or praise to motivate, your words, actions, and concern fall on deaf ears when someone is in a semi-slide.

As the wrestler in the semi-slides is determined to self-destruct.

Your words, actions, and inspiration will prove to be of no match against their self-sabotage.

The brain of the wrestler in the semi-slide isn't functioning the way it should because it can't reconcile the magnitude of their recent loss.

The only way out of a wrestling semi-slide is for the wrestler to be present in the present, to find gratitude and to reset a new goal.

If the wrestler who experienced a traumatic loss in the semi-finals were able to remain present in the present, he would have beaten his next two opponents and capped his loss at one.

If the wrestler found gratitude, however hard that may have been at the time, their brain would have refocused itself to find the good and allow the wrestler to rebuild again.

If after the initial loss the wrestler reset a new goal to take 3rd place, he would have capped the loss at one.

Inside the torturous experience of the wrestling semi-slide is one of the most important life lessons the sport of wrestling will ever teach.

Have you ever witnessed a life-slide?

Or perhaps experience one yourself?

Have you ever known a person who just experienced a traumatic event in life?

Who suffered a severe loss?

A person whose brain can't reconcile the event that just took place?

Or a person who is addicted?

As any person who has ever attempted to reason with anyone who has, or is, knows, it is one of the most helpless feelings one could ever experience in life.

No matter what you say, no matter what you do, no matter if you use fear or praise to motivate, your words, actions, and concern fall on deaf ears when someone is in a life-slide.

As the person in the life-slides brain isn't functioning the way it should in the present situation because it can't reconcile the magnitude of their recent loss.

It is determined to self-destruct.

Your words, actions, and inspiration will prove to be of no match against their self-sabotage.

Until
They reconcile the event in their minds, by staying present in the present,
They find gratitude,
And they reset a new goal.

After a traumatic loss in life, it is often difficult to reconcile the event in your mind, but being present in the present gives you the best opportunity to.

As it is never the first wave that drowns you, it is the inability to recover from its force that allows the smaller second, third, and fourth waves to do the deed.

If the second, third, or fourth waves were taken by themselves, they would have been easily handled and proven to have been of no danger.

Their real danger is in their immediacy after the first wave redirected one's attention and forced one to lose focus.

Finding gratitude is the key to life.

Appreciation is the bridge from suffering to gratitude.

Gratitude is the fertile land where love flourishes.

And love is the greatest achievement in life.

After a traumatic loss whether in wrestling or life, the way you stop one loss from beating you twice is that you remain present in the present, you find gratitude, and you reset a new goal.

Unfortunately, no amount of the care given to a person in a life-slide by the people who love them will have a permanent impact on them until they do.

Every person will get back to the present, find gratitude, and reset a new goal in their own time, at their own pace.

And when they do, they will rebuild.

Rule #67
It Has to Hurt

Wisdom
Is nothing more than
Healed pain.
Robert Gary-Lee

You set out to achieve greatness, and you have come up short.

You met your match.

You now realize that you gave it your all, and your all just wasn't enough.

And it hurts.

It hurts badly.

Worse than anything you have ever felt before.

There is only one thing left to do,

Trust in the process.

It has to hurt.

For the hurt that festers in your soul gets converted to drive, hard work, and ambition.

All vital ingredients needed to propel you to the next level.

There are only 15 wrestlers per year that win their last four matches of the season.

All the rest will end their season with a loss.

But don't let a loss defeat you.

Especially twice.

You will learn more from your losses than you ever will from your wins.

Let the loss hurt.

When it hurts, it means you care.

When you care, you will figure it out.

Rededicate yourself.

I needn't remind you that you didn't set out to achieve something ordinary.

You set out to accomplish something extraordinary.

Therefore, it is going to require an extraordinary effort.

One, which separates yourself from others.

And those others, are hungry wrestlers who are willing and able to go through physical and mental torture.

So, stand back up.

First, look back, and see how far you've come.

Then look ahead and see how much further there is to go.

I guarantee the shorter distance is the one ahead of you.

Discouragement is a dream chaser.

Shelve the feelings of discouragement and focus on the work.

Wrestling is the greatest sport on earth for the sole reason that the people who are willing to work will see success.

It is not a matter of if,

But when.

Be relentless in the pursuit of your goal.

Make your will the strongest part of your makeup.

There is a reason why you are going through what you are.

Believe that.

Everything happens for a reason; else it would have happened differently.

There is something that you need to learn to prepare you for what is to come.

Inspect what that reason may be.

Embrace it.

Understand there is still more to be learned.

Concentrate on progress and not perfection.

Count the times you gave 100% for 6 minutes this year.

Then top that effort next year.

That's it.

It's that simple.

You will get there.

Hurt is an indispensable part of the formula for greatness.

A loss is not where the journey ends.

It is where the initiation into greatness begins.

Pain is painful.

It is also necessary.

RULE #68
PAIN IS YOUR GREATEST TEACHER

These pains that you feel are messengers,
Listen to them.
Rumi

"That's going to hurt for a long time."

"I don't know if he'll ever recover."

One hears these words every year at the State wrestling tournament after a wrestler loses an important match.

Some wrestlers do recover from significant losses, and some do not.

The ones that do recover use their pain to motivate them to take action to address an area that needs fixing.

The ones that don't recover are the ones who do not use their pain to motivate them but rather attempt to hide, diminish, or ignore it.

****

After my High School wrestling career was over, and I didn't accomplish the goals I set out to, I vowed I would never let my sons wrestle.

I never wanted them to experience the pain that I experienced from this sport.

I was wrong in my protective thinking.

Pain is invaluable to experience.

****

Famous American Actress, Cicely Tyson tells a story,

"I once ran across a young child who did not know who Dr. Martin Luther King was.

You know, when we were fighting for rights, we did not want them to go through what we had to go through. We were trying to make it possible for them to use their energies and their talents to do other things to help humanity.

And because of that, we left them nothing to fight for; they didn't understand what it meant."

****

Pain is painful.

It is also necessary.

Pain is a motivator for one to act.

Pain is the stimulus of change, improvement, and correction.

Pain is an indicator that something is not right.

Pain forces one to address a situation that needs changing and never repeating.

Listen to your pain,

Absorb it,

Let it soak in.

Then let it motivate you to take the corrective action to eliminate its presence.

Pain is a necessary evil which must be endured to receive the rewards one desires.

RULE #69
PAIN ENDURED
IS STRENGTH STORED

We acquire the strength we have overcome.
Emerson

What makes wrestlers different from many people is
their understanding of what
Mihaly Csikszentmuhalvi so profoundly wrote,

"Of all the virtues we can learn,
No trait is more useful,
More essential for survival,
And more likely to improve the quality of life
Then the ability to transform adversity into an
enjoyable challenge."

Wrestlers understand that pain is a gateway to
achievement.

Pain is a necessary evil which must be endured to
receive the reward one desires.

Pain is a separator of people during battle.

We have all heard the expression,

"No pain, no gain."

It is a cliché because it's true.

Nothing worth achieving comes easy.

Everything worth achieving will have trials and tribulations attached, dark moments of doubts that will push you to the edge of your beliefs where you must decide whether to endure or quit.

Every time you endure the doubt, you store some strength.

Every time you quit, you lose strength, and it then becomes easier to quit the next time.

Have you ever noticed that a wrestler will always choose the most painful option?

Why?

Are they just masochists that love pain?

No, quite the opposite.

Wrestlers crave the desired outcome more than they despise pain, and they understand that the only way to get the desired outcome is to embrace the pain.

Pain is a toll booth to success.

Pay the toll and store the strength.

Muhammad Ali said it best when he said,

"I hated every minute of training.
But I said to myself, don't quit.
Suffer now and live the rest of your life as a champion."

Pain endured is strength stored.

Somewhere inside the rubble,
The Seed of Something Greater
will appear to you one day.

Rule #70
Never Lose the Bruises
From Your Greatest Loss

Turn your wounds,
Into wisdom.
Oprah Winfrey

Use your bruises.

Keep them visible to yourself.

They are a reminder of the trials and tribulations and pain that you were willing to endure to achieve your goal.

There are losses, and then there are losses.

Some losses are easy to overcome.

And some losses rock your world.

They disrupt your course.

They alter the axis on which your world spins.

They disrupt your gravity.

They send you in a free fall.

In my experience, these "rock your world" losses come every 7-10 years in life.

Their effects on you are dramatic.

Dramatic enough for you to feel them constantly, to have them factored into every risk decision you ever make and for them to be with you always.

Their effects do wear down over time, though.

It has been my experience just about the time their effects start to fade, another new 7-10-year, "rock your world" loss will appear.

These 7-10-year, "rock your world" losses are very difficult to understand and comprehend.

I know it doesn't feel like it, but ultimately, they are there to guide you.

And most importantly, they come with a gift.

The Universal Law of Reciprocity says that being that the loss took something of value from you, it must give you back "The Seed of Something Greater" in return.

After all the smoke has cleared look for "The Seed of Something Greater."

It will be there.

It's a Universal Law.

One day, when you are breezing through the rubble of your life, "The Seed of Something Greater" will appear.

The seed will contain a way of keeping the spirit of your loss alive.

What you do with "The Seed of Something Greater" will be up to you.

You can decide to ignore it.
Or you can decide to plant it.

Choose wisely.

The future quality of your life lies in the balance.

Arriving at your destination can be as dangerous as quitting.

RULE #71
ALWAYS BE IN RELENTLESS PURSUIT
OF EXCELLENCE

Roads were made for journeys
Not destinations.
Confucius

Always be in pursuit of becoming the best version of yourself.

Dream.

As it requires you to be excellent.

When you decide to go after your dream, there will be only two times when you will not be in relentless pursuit of excellence.

One is if you decide to quit, which you will never do, and the second is when you achieve your goal and arrive at your destination.

Quitting is common and will not be discussed in this book because I know you will never quit.

Rest if you must, but never quit.

The trickier occurrence of when you will not be in relentless pursuit of excellence is when you achieve your goal and arrive at your intended destination.

Arriving at your destination can be as dangerous as quitting.

The reason being, both quitting and arriving, have the same result.

In both cases, you are no longer in relentless pursuit of excellence.

It is extremely important after arriving at your intended destination to set a new goal, to go on a new journey.

After you arrive, celebrate, rest, and then get back to being in relentless pursuit of excellence.

Life is a series of journeys and destinations.

"Little by little, one travels far,"
Bilbo Baggins reminded us in "The Hobbit."

RULE #72
IT IS SIMPLE
BUT NOT EASY

What I believe is not believed by everyone,
And is not practiced by everyone who believes it.
Pat Schneider

Never confuse simple and easy.

Simple is easy to understand but hard to execute.

Figuring out the path to success is simple.

Walking the path is hard.

The execution is always the hard part.

The execution requires sacrifice and discipline.

The execution requires precision planning and prioritizing.

The execution requires massive work, insane boredom, and extreme loneliness.

The execution requires you to feel the acute pain of failure and requires you to grapple a few rounds with self-doubt and discouragement.

Everyone wants to be a champion.
What they don't want is to live the lifestyle and endure the pain that is necessary to become one.

Have you ever witnessed a wrestler come up with an off-season plan?

Most execute the plan while their mood is still right, but once the mystique of having a big goal has worn off and the actual grueling work is required, they fall to the wayside.

Others, the champions, continue to execute their plan well past the point of being in vogue to do so.

They do things others are not willing to do.
That is why they get what others are not able to get.

Never confuse simple and easy.

The difference between simple and easy is the work.

And work is hard.

Rule #73
Don't Let Victory Defeat You

There is a kind of success worse than failure,
And a kind of failure
Worth all the success in the world.
Jean Cocteau
Paris Album

It is much harder to stay on top than it is to get to the top.

Granted, getting to the top is extremely difficult, but when you arrive, it is quite common to forget how you got there, to overlook the little things that you concentrated on, the focus you had, the desire that was inside of you.

Victory can become your worst enemy for future success if you let it.

Don't.

Understand what it took to become victorious. Reminisce with the loneliness, the sacrifice, the exhausting work that it took to become victorious.

Never lose sight of the work and sacrifice it took to get where you are and every day after your victory ask yourself,

"Am I working harder now after my victory than I did before my victory?"

"Am I living the same lifestyle as I did before I became a champion?"

"Have I set a new goal, a bigger goal?"

If all the answers to the above questions are yes, then you have a chance of staying on top.

If any answer to the above questions is no, then you won't.

It is that simple.

You will find that the formula of staying on top is the same as the one that is needed to get to the top.

The formula doesn't change.
So, if you want to stay on top, you shouldn't change either.

Rule #74
Be Humble
Or Be Ready To Be Humbled

There ain't been a horse that can't be rode.
Nor a cowboy
Who can't be throwed.
An old Texas saying

My favorite photo is one of two wrestlers embracing in the center of the circle after a grueling post-season match.

Both are sweaty and tired.

One is victorious; the other is not.

The victorious wrestler is cupping the head of the other wrestler with his hand bringing it down to lay on his shoulder.

The other wrestler is holding back tears.

Not baby tears, but the tears one has when one is physically exhausted after given everything they had and still have been cruelly shown defeat instead of victory.

What makes this photo my favorite photo is the compassion the victorious wrestler shows the other.

What I haven't told you is that I know both wrestlers in the photo.

I watched both develop and grow over the years.

I watched both push each other to their limits in club practice, where they were workout partners.

Now they are meeting in the postseason.

And only one wrestler can advance to the postseason.

The compassion the victorious wrestler shows in the photo comes from knowing how it feels to be on the other side of victory after dedicating your life and fully expecting to be on the right side.

The compassion seethes from the photo as one can see the victorious wrestler has a conflicted look.

A look of heartache that he was the one who ended the other wrestlers' dream combined with a conflicted look of "thank you."

"Thank you for being my rival."

"Thank you for pushing me to the point where I have realized my dream."

"Thank you for being a great competitor."

"Thank you for bringing out the best in me."

There is another look the victorious wrestler has in the photo.

A look that says,
"I wish we both could experience victory, that we could both advance, both go to states, but today is my turn. Keep the faith. I know you will use this loss to one day have your day too, that I am certain of."

There is a mutual respect that wrestlers have for each other.

They understand the sacrifice.
They understand the lifestyle.

One of the greatest attributes a wrestler can have is humility to his opponent after victory over him.

****

In the long run, a loss that makes you humble
will be better than a win that makes you arrogant.

This sport is the most humbling in the world.

You can do everything right; give everything you
have and still not achieve what you set out to
achieve.

An injury, a bad call, one second on either side of a
takedown on the line, getting a cold at the wrong
time of the year can all affect the outcome of any
match at any time. And it only takes one match to
evaporate your dream.

Knowing you have no control over at least 10% of
the stuff that happens creates an understanding of
the vulnerability that every wrestler must live and
come to terms with.

Even elite wrestlers.

Humble wrestlers understand that the difference
between victory and an off-season of mental torture
is so small.

They too may have experienced being so close to victory in this sport only to have their hearts ripped from their chests.

And they remember that feeling.

And they wouldn't want anyone they respect ever to have to experience that feeling.

That is compassion.

Compassion is the greatest part of humility.

There have been times where I have seen wrestlers take the opposite approach.

Being brash, trash-talking to their opponents after victory, degrading them after beating them.

Only to have their opponents use that disrespected feeling as fuel to train to come back and beat them in a more important spot.

Life is the same way.

Just exchange being humble with being grateful.

When one is grateful for their life, the people in it, their surroundings they give off an aura of blessing and attraction.

When one compares their life to others, they give off a sense of dissatisfaction.

And the Universe senses that.

Always be humble.

It exudes gratitude.

And gratitude is the path to love.

And love is the greatest victory of all.

Rule #75
Respect the Sport
And the Sport Will Respect You

Knowledge will give you power,
But character respect.
Bruce Lee

The Merriam-Webster dictionary defines respect as,

"A feeling of deep admiration for someone or something elicited by their abilities, qualities, or achievements."

If you as a wrestler do the work necessary to become successful, whether success is reached, or not, people involved in this sport will notice.

If you as a wrestler develop the qualities that are necessary to go to battle against adversity and your integrity in times of turmoil remains true, people involved in this sport will honor you.

If you are one of the lucky ones that achieve great things in this sport, the people in this sport will applaud you.

Understand, achieving great things is measured by the distance from where you started to where you finished.

It is not measured by standing at the highest point on a podium for a few seconds.

Some of the greatest achievements in the sport of wrestling occur by those whose measured distance is unknown by others.

In those situations, you will earn the highest form of respect.

Your own.

Rule #76
Don't Take the Bait

Not all that glitters
Is gold.

It is happening more and more in this era.

Wrestlers who take the bait.

One wrestler dangling his leg out in front of him,
unprotected to entice his opponent to take it.

As soon as the wrestler takes the bait, he finds
himself spladled on his back.

Match over.

****

Imagine a conversation between two fish.

One fish says to another, "Hey, do you see that juicy
worm over there?"

The other fish says, "Stay away from that worm;
I heard there is a hook in it."

"I know there is, everyone knows there is, but I think I can eat around the hook," the first fish says. "Too risky, I've heard stories of other fish trying to eat that worm, and they always get hooked," the other fish says.

"I'm going to try it anyway, my friend asked me to go with him later, and it sounds like fun.

He says it is the best-tasting worm he has ever eaten.

What harm could it do to nibble on the part of the worm furthest from the hook?

I'm not stupid enough to bite at the worm nearest the hook," the first fish says.

The next day the fish came back with a glowing account of his night.

"You see, I told you, I'm okay. You don't know what you are missing, that was the most delicious worm I ever had.

I had the time of my life last night.

You should come with me. I'm going back again tonight."
The first fish wisely stands his ground and declines his friends offer.

The two fish drift apart.

Day after day, the other fish goes back to eat more of the worm.

Day after day, the deliciousness of the worm decreases.

Day after day, the amount left of the worm decreases.

One day the two fish bump into each other out of the blue.

The one fish barely recognizes the other.

And once again the other fish invites his friend to go with him.

Once again, he declines.

The fish goes back on his own, and when he gets there, there is only a very small piece of worm left.

And it is sitting right on the point of the hook.

Desperate for the taste of the once delicious worm, the fish does the one thing he swore he would never be stupid enough to do,

He ignores the risk and goes after the piece of the worm closest to the hook,

He bites down hard.

And gets hooked.

Rule #77
Your Nights Must Be Friends
With Your Days

No man, for any considerable period,
Can wear one face to himself
And another to the multitude,
Without finally getting bewildered
As to which may be the true.

Nathaniel Hawthorne
The Scarlet Letter

Harmony between one's life on the mat and off the mat is a key determining factor for their continued success.

The ironic part is the more successful one is on the mat, the greater the distance they put between themselves and their competition, the greater the tendency it is for them to utilize their time in contrast to the way they did which created their success.

We all know the fairytale of "The Tortoise and the Hare."

The Tortoise could never imagine the Hare ever catching up to him; he was faster, more talented, he worked harder.

Until he didn't.

When the Tortoise stopped working and started utilizing his time in contrast to how he did when he acquired his lead, he opened the door for the Hare's victory.

****

"Nothing good happens after midnight."

How many times have you heard that in your life?

Midnight is the hypothetical line in the sand that identifies where your focus is.

What you focus on will get amplified by the attention you pay it.

If your day ends with hard work and it is important for you to put in another hard-working day tomorrow, then your focus must be on the time before midnight.

Once your focus starts becoming on the time after midnight, you are now sharing the focus reserved to build greatness with all the things that go against you from obtaining greatness.

And you start to drift from living in harmony to living in conflict.

Once conflict occurs, chaos ensues.

It is much easier to stay disciplined than it is to get discipline back into your life again.

Imagine you are in a boat with nine other rowers.

You start with all ten rowers all rowing in the same direction.

There is harmony.

The speed is fast, the pace is quick, you are each motivating each other, and there is a feeling of synchronicity. You make each other better.

Now imagine if out of the blue one rower starts to row in the opposite direction.

Conflict occurs.

At first, the force and momentum of the nine rowers still rowing in the same direction are too much for the one rower rowing in the opposite direction to overcome.

But slowly but surely there will be resentment from the nine rowers who are doing all the work toward the one who is now going against what they want to accomplish.

Now imagine if that one rower starts talking some of the other nine rowers into joining him.

And after comparing the hard work they are doing to the perceived fun it would be to rebel, they join him.

And before you know it that once harmonious boat is now in chaos, five rowers are now rowing in opposite directions.

The boat has come to a halt and is not going anywhere.

Eventually, more rowers will join the other side, and the original direction will now be redirected and outweighed by rowers rowing in the wrong direction.

And the boat will start to give up ground.

****

In life, having discipline is good.

It maintains harmony.

It eliminates conflict.

Remember, "If you chase two rabbits, both will escape."

For how others see you is not nearly as important as how the Universe sees you.

RULE #78
THE UNIVERSE IS WATCHING
WHEN NO ONE IS THERE

The fight is won or lost far away from witnesses
Behind the lines,
In the gym,
And out there on the road,
Long before I dance under those lights.
Muhammed Ali

Applause can't be your motivator.

As a wrestler, you train in seclusion, you live with social discipline, and you compete in an empty gym.

Applause can't be your motivator.

The reasons why you compete must stem from the inside out, not the outside in.

There are no large crowds, no big media following, no social or professional pedestals for wrestlers.

But there is a deep inner worth.

****

In life after wrestling, applause can't be your motivator.

For if it is, you will miss out on the most powerful dynamic,

The dynamic of secretly doing something for someone who has no way of repaying you.

When you do something for someone who can never repay you, and no one sees you do it, always remember, the Universe is watching.

And that is the greatest audience in the world.

For how others see you is not nearly as important as how the Universe sees you.

Rule #79
Live Your Life In Such a Way That People Root For Your Success

Be humble enough to know
That you're not better than anybody,
And wise enough to know
That you're different from the rest.

The way that you carry yourself,

The way that you present yourself,

The way that you compete,

The way that you interact with your allies and rivals,

The way that you win,

The way that you temporarily lose,

The way that you care,

The way that you dare,

The way that you strive,

The way that you fall,

The way that you get back up,

The way that you dream,
The way that you recover,

It all goes through a visual filter in every person's brain to determine two things.

Whether they like and trust you.

And when they both like and trust you, they will root for you.

They will root for you as one of their own.

It is not whether you have or get things in life or sport, but it is about the humanity of the story others can admire; how you lived, how they can relate to your humanity that causes them to root for you.

When someone sees someone else live admirably, they take notice and become a fan.

The ironic thing is my experience in life has shown me that overcoming hardship is the prerequisite to how others see you living admirably.

It is how you handle that hardship that stands out.

Why?

Because hardship is a hard ship to steer.

And as humans, we admire when another human steer that hard ship out of the eye of the storm and back into tranquil waters.

That is worth rooting for.

That is when you will get your greatest applause.

There is a possibility, heck, maybe even a probability, that you will give everything you have and not get the reward you sought after.

RULE #80
THERE IS NO GUARANTEE OF SUCCESS

Can a man still be brave if he's afraid?
That is the only time a man can be brave.
George RR Martin
Game of Thrones

It takes time, experience, and pain to acquire knowledge.

Certain knowledge must be realized at the right time as if it is revealed too soon it may not be able to be handled properly.

There is a point in a wrestler's career when they will come to a fork in the road.

The All-In fork.

They weigh the cost of going all in verse the reward of what they want and determine if they are willing to pay the price.

They determine that they are willing.

So, they take the fork and go "All-In."

They then go on to do everything right,
they become the best at what they do.

They hold up their end of the bargain.

But all the information wasn't given to them at the time.

Key information was withheld.

The "All-In" fork contained a lie of omission.

The lie being that even if you do everything right,

Even if you are the best at what you do,

Even if you have done everything to get every advantage,

Even if you have won before,

There is no guarantee of success.

That is the reality.

And that changes things.

Not everyone who goes "All-In" factors going "All-In" and then not getting the reward.

If they did, some would elect not to proceed.

Thus, the reason for the lie of omission from the "All-In" fork.

Later, during their journey, after some time and a series of setbacks, a wrestler will face a new fork in the road.

A more truthful fork.

A much scarier fork.

The "All-In-With-No-Guarantee-Of-Success" fork.

At that fork the wrestler will be asked to recommit to the "All-In" fork with the additional information of that even if you go "All-In" and hold up your end of the bargain, this may not work out the way you have planned.

That is a scary thought.
It takes a brave person to proceed down this new fork knowing the whole truth.

There is a possibility, heck, maybe even a probability, that you will give everything you have and not get the reward you sought after.

When one reaches this part of the fork's road, there is enlightenment.

When traveling down this new fork one is given the knowledge and realization of the Universal Law of,

"The reward you seek may not be the reward you receive."

And something great happens.

They trust in the Universe that the outcome that they will receive will be the outcome their life needs.

Mahatma Gandhi said it best,

"It's the action, not the fruit of the action, that's important.

You have to do the right thing.
It may not be in your power, may not be in your time, that there'll be any fruit.

But that doesn't mean you stop doing the right thing.

You may never know what results come from your action.

But if you do nothing, there will be no result."

There always is a reward for taking the journey.

It just may not be the one you sought.

It may just prove to be more powerful than you could ever wish for.

> *There are many deserving people in this world.*

Rule #81
You Don't Get What You Deserve
You Only Get What You Earn

Do, or do not.
There is no try.
Star Wars

Being able to execute in the big spot is a sign of a champion.

Imagine going undefeated all season, 50-0 and then losing in the state finals to a wrestler with a record of 40-10.

On paper, it would have seemed that you had deserved to win.

But championships aren't won on paper.

They're won in the circle.

And every time you step into the circle, the past is wiped clean, and the only thing that matters is the next six minutes.

There is one thing that I don't agree with.

All coaches give a similar rally speech which goes something like this,

"Nobody deserves it more than us,"

"Nobody worked harder than us,"

"Nobody wants it more than us."

That is simply not true.

At the elite level, if you didn't work hard, you wouldn't be there, and everybody wants it.

The truth is what differentiates the champions from 2nd place finishers is being able to execute in the big spot.

To be able to have your best performance at the right moment.

There are many deserving people in this world.

The people who achieve are the ones who execute in a big spot.

RULE #82
BE MORE PROUD
THAN DISAPPOINTED

We should not judge people
By their peak of excellence;
But by the distance, they have traveled
From the point where they started.
Henry Ward Beecher

Many times in my life as a parent of an athlete, I've had to catch myself, to put things into proper perspective.

To keep the big picture in focus.

To not get caught up in the quest for short term success and to keep the end goal in mind.

It is so easy to be disappointed, to get down, to compare all the sacrifices that were made to get to the point of victory and then to lose the victory when so close.

Luckily, due to previous adversity in my life I can immediately change perspective. And I when I do I realize all the tremendous hard work, effort and commitment it took just to be in the position to succeed and the person my son is becoming in the process. It is then that I become more proud of my son than disappointed in his lost opportunity.

And when I do, everything changes.

I see life through a new lens.

A lens of gratitude and pride.

The world looks magnificent through the lens of gratitude and pride.

And the relationship with my son blossoms.

It wasn't until after my both my sons became New York State champions did I realize what I thought was my end goal for them, to win the state championship, wasn't my real end goal.

My real end goal was for my sons, while in pursuit of wrestling excellence, to acquire the attributes and characteristics necessary to prepare them to live a loving and productive life as a kind and caring human being.

RULE #83
TRUST IN THE PROCESS

These are the days that must happen to you.
Walt Whitman

I won't make-believe that I was this great wrestler.

I wasn't.

But I do know a little something about dedicating your life to something and feeling unrewarded.

When I was younger, I gave six years of my life to this sport, and I never got to stand on the top step of the podium in the tournament I set out to do so in.

I walked away, feeling like I didn't achieve what I set out to do in the sport I loved.

I hated the sport for not reciprocating the love I had for it.

I left the sport feeling that my six years wasn't worth it.

That it was a total waste of time and effort.

It took me many years to realize that even though I never accomplished my goals in wrestling, wrestling accomplished its goals in me.

They call wrestling the greatest sport on earth for a reason.

It just took me twenty-six years to realize why.

You see, you are on a journey.

Right now, you think the journey is about winning wrestling matches.

One day, many years from now, you will realize it's about so much more.

Silently this sport is building within you everything you will need to be successful in your life.

But only if you allow it to.

Now, you only see plateaus and loss and unfulfilled dreams.

It all seems like chaos.

But the lessons within the chaos are important.

More important than winning.

One day you will understand that.

If I can convince you of only one thing,
let it be this,

You need to trust in the process.

You have to trust the work you are completely
immersing yourself in, is either going to produce
your desired result or equip you with the tools
needed to conquer a more important future
endeavor, one you neither understand or are
currently aware of right now.

I believe the lucky ones in this sport,
which I consider myself to be one of,
get something of far greater value than standing on
top of a podium for a few seconds.

They get a way to live life.
And that lasts their whole life, not just the length of
an awards ceremony.

Understand this, there will be a time in your life
when you will be in the fight of your life, facing an
opponent much bigger than you, and you will be
called upon to win something much more important
than a wrestling match.

Not only for yourself, but for your family.

One day your family may be faced with death,
a divorce, or a diagnosis.

The one thing I know for sure in life is your
family will be much better prepared to win that
fight, with you having wrestled.

Wrestling is about learning how to fight,
to be able to beat what life is going to throw at you.

You are doing a great job.
Forget about plateaus and getting to the next level.

Just trust in the process

And I can assure you,
You will be rewarded in the end.

RULE #84
TRUST IN THE UNIVERSE
IT KNOWS WHAT IT IS DOING

Sometimes the Universe turns your life upside down
To teach you to live right side up.

"Why is this happening to me?"

We have all said this to ourselves at one point in time.

I have learned to adjust this question slightly.

Whenever I find myself saying,

"Why is this happening to me?"

I adjust it to,

"This is happening for me."

This slight adjustment is based on the writing of Marcus Aurelius when he said,

"No experience goes wasted.
True understanding is to see the events of life in this
way.
Truly whatever arises in life
Is the right material to bring about your growth,
And the growth of those around you.
Everything contains some special purpose
And a hidden blessing."

After hearing the slight adjustment, my mind
immediately goes into detective mode to find the
jewel life has hidden inside the mess it has thrown at
me.

I truly believe the Universe knows what it is doing.

We need to become more in tune with it.

Trust what happens in your life is what your life
needs for reasons unknown to only the Universe.

RULE #85
THE REWARD YOU SEEK
MAY NOT BE THE REWARD YOU RECEIVE

What I am looking for
Is not out there,
It is in me.

Helen Keller

The best way to teach someone something is to have them think they are learning something else.

And allow it to dawn on them that life parallels the problems your subconscious mind is working on.

All they must do is apply the lessons they have learned elsewhere to solving their problem.

"Wash the car."

"Paint the fence."

Are perfect examples from the Karate Kid.

Originally, Daniel thought Mr. Miyagi was putting him to work doing meaningless chores around his house solely for Mr. Miyagi's benefit.

Over time, it dawned on Daniel that the chores Mr. Miyagi made him master were parallel to the exact skill Daniel needed to solve his problem that his subconscious mind was working on; how to defend himself against Johnny.

Every day there are chores the Universe makes us go through, makes us experience and master, that we believe are meaningless which turn out to be cleverly crafted lessons designed to give us the answers to our questions our subconscious mind is working on.

For me, for the better part of my life up until the time I became an adult, I believed I was mastering the skills needed to accomplish my vision of becoming a New York State Champion.

But the Universe had a bigger vision.

Instead of rewarding me with a few moments standing on the top podium as a state champion, it rewarded me with a way to live the rest of my life.

It took me many years to realize this.
It is one of the greatest realizations I have ever taken from this sport.

Ultimately, wrestling for me was not about winning a state championship. At the time, I needed to believe it was so I would continue to learn all the lessons I needed to learn, with all my heart and soul, to prepare me for life.

Wrestling is about supplying you with a lifestyle to be successful in every aspect of life.

I truly believe if I had won the State Championship, it might never have dawned on me what the Universe was doing; ultimately preparing me for life.

In the end, the reward I sought, becoming a New York State champion, was not the reward I received.

The reward I received, becoming prepared for life, was so much greater.

At the time, I had to believe the reward I sought was my end goal, but it was just a parallel life experience.

Allow the sport, through its peaks and valleys, trials and tribulations, through its disappointment and its glory, chisel you into the best version of yourself.

RULE #86
BECOME THE BEST VERSION OF YOURSELF

It is not our abilities
That show who we truly are,
It is our choices.
Dumbledore
Harry Potter and the Chamber of Secrets

No job interviewer ever asked a potential hire,

"How is your single leg?" in a job interview.

Even though many employers seek to hire former wrestlers.

That is because the qualities the sport of wrestling teaches, hard work, commitment, dedication, perseverance, overcoming adversity, are much more important than the actual techniques one acquires from the sport.

The application off the mat is much more valuable than the one on the mat.

Use the sport of wrestling to acquire the qualities needed to improve the quality of life of those around you, including your own.

Allow the sport, through its peaks and valleys, trials and tribulations, through its disappointment and its glory, chisel you into the best version of yourself on the mat.

Then choose to apply the qualities you learned while seeking greatness on the mat to your life off the mat.

That is the true purpose of this sport.

That is what this great sport is all about.

To acquire a lifestyle which will transform you into the best version of yourself in life.

RULE #87
HAVE GREAT BALANCE

I contain multitudes.
Walt Whitman

You must give it your all,

But it can never have all of you or be all you are.

Undoubtedly, in your quest to become your best, you may need to borrow from other areas of your life.

Sometimes on onerous terms.

Thus, becoming unbalanced and overweighted in pursuit of your goal.

Make sure this is only temporary.

Elite wrestlers have great balance.

Especially in their lives.

Remember to repay in full the other areas of your life you have borrowed from to become great.

Wrestling, like life, is not only about the body,
it is also about the mind, the spirit, and other people.

Wrestling, like life, is not only about you,
it is about the people who have sacrificed for you
and the people who have sacrificed with you.
It is about the family who has supported you and
the coaches who have invested their belief and
experience in you.

With so many people doing so much to see you
succeed, remember to acknowledge and reciprocate
their kindness.

Find Gratitude.

Work Hard.
Stay humble.
Pay kindness forward.

Balance.
Mind.
Body.
Spirit.

Achievement.

Rule #88
Your Journey
Is Specifically Designed for You

Not I, nor anyone else
Can travel that road for you.
You must travel it yourself.
Walt Whitman

There is a picture that sits behind my dresser in my bedroom stored between my dresser and the wall.

Every so often, I come across it.

Every time I do, I wonder,

"What if I got that two count?"

The picture I am referring to is a picture of me in my last high school wrestling match having lat dropped my rival but unable to have kept him on his back long enough to get a two count which would have won the match.

I got a one count.

And I lost by one point.

I have always wondered, "What if I got that two count?"

For years I remained immature about the situation and felt cheated,

"How didn't the ref get down in time to properly count back points?"

That one second haunted me for a long time.

That one second took twenty-six years for me to get over.

The significance of that one second to my life took me twenty-six years to fully understand.

After twenty-six years, I finally got it.

Life doesn't happen to you,

It happens for you.

My winning a New York State Wrestling Championship wasn't my journey.

You see if I had gotten that two count my life wouldn't be the same.

If I had got that two count, without a doubt, I would have gone to a different college.

Having gone to a different college,
I more than likely would have stopped dating the girl I was dating at the time, which turned out to be my future wife.

And without marrying my wife, we would not have had any of our kids.

If I would have gotten that two count, I wouldn't have the people in life that I now love the most.

My life wouldn't be as I know it.

I would never trade any member of my family for a state championship.

Not even for 4 state championships.

I believe life happened for me when I got that one count, even though I couldn't comprehend the loss at the time.

Today I believe I am exactly where I was meant to be.
I believe I have become the person I was meant to be.

I believe adversity and struggle have shaped and carved me into who I am.

I am the best version of myself.

And I have the sport of wrestling, and a one count in my final high school match to thank for that.

I believe my journey was specifically designed for me.

I also believe that you, too, have a journey specifically designed for you.

You may not understand it; it may take years to appear, but I assure you, the journey that is awaiting you, the one that is designed specifically for you is far greater than the journey you currently desire.

Retired Oakland A's pitcher Barry Zito on reflecting looking back on his sports career and comparing it to life after it said,

"Beyond all of the achievements, the single thing that fulfills me today is the acceptance of myself as a worthy and valuable person, regardless of what my stature or position in the world was on a given day of my sports career."

And that is the real goal.

The one the Universe is teaching you by tricking you into thinking your athletic efforts are for something else, that they are about glory on the mat.

They are not.

They are about preparing you to live a glorious life of the mat.

Chapter 00

In the writing of this book, I have examined what the sport of wrestling has taught me and how I have applied what I have learned to my life.

These are my lessons.

The ones that are valuable to me.

It is my wish that they, in some small way, help make every wrestler's life off the mat better with their application.

Wrestling is a fraternity, and I consider all who have ever wrestled my teammates.

This book is my attempt at being a great partner.

Thank you for investing your time.

JohnA Passaro

FOR QUANTITY DISCOUNTS OF THIS
BOOK

FOR WRESTLING TEAMS, OR
WRESTLING CLUBS

PLEASE EMAIL

JOHNAPASSARO@ICLOUD.COM

CONTACT INFO

STORE - www.johnapassarostore.com

BLOG - www.johnapassaroblog.com

EMAIL – johnapassaro@icloud.com

FACEBOOK – www.facebook.com/john.passaro.50

FACEBOOK -
www.facebook.com/JohnA.Passaro.Wrestling.with.Life/

TWITTER - @johnapassaro

www.johnapassarostore.com

FOR ALL PUBLISHED WORKS BY

JohnA Passaro

PLEASE GO TO:

www.johnapassarostore.com

Made in the USA
Monee, IL
16 January 2023

25395951R00179